CAMPAIGN • 231

NEZ PERCE 1877

The last fight

ROBERT FORCZYK

ILLUSTRATED BY PETER DENNIS
Series editor Marcus Cowper

First published in Great Britain in 2011 by Osprey Publishing,
Midland House, West Way, Botley, Oxford OX2 0PH, UK
44-02 23rd St, Suite 219, Long Island City, NY 11101, USA

E-mail: info@ospreypublishing.com

A CIP catalog record for this book is available from the British Library.

ISBN: 978 1 84908 191 7

e book ISBN: 978 1 84908 192 4

Editorial by Ilios Publishing Ltd, Oxford, UK (www.iliospublishing.com)
Page layout by: The Black Spot
Index by Alison Worthington
Typeset in Sabon and Myriad Pro
Maps by Bounford.com
3D bird's-eye views by The Black Spot
Battlescene illustrations by Peter Dennis
Originated by PDQ Media
Printed in China through Worldprint

10 11 12 13 14   10 9 8 7 6 5 4 3 2 1

ACKNOWLEDGMENTS

I would like to thank Mr. Fred Poyner IV from the Washington State
Historical Society; Bob Smith from the US Cavalry Museum at Fort Riley,
Kansas; David Miller from the American History Museum of the Smithsonian
Institute; as well as the staff of the Library of Congress.

DEDICATION

This volume is dedicated to First Lieutenant Edward Theller, Company
G/21st Infantry, KIA on June 17, 1877, Second Lieutenant Sevier M. Rains,
Company L/1st Cavalry, KIA on July 3, 1877 and First Lieutenant James
Bradley, Company B/7th Infantry, KIA on August 9, 1877. These young men
– all but forgotten now – gave their lives in the service of their nation.

AUTHOR'S NOTE

Unlike other publications on the subject of the Nez Perce War, I do not
intend to use racist terms such as "Whites" to refer to American settlers.
Nor do I intend to use the modern term "Native American," since the
Non-Treaty Nez Perce did not consider themselves as Americans in 1877.
I will use the terms Nez Perce and Nimiipuu somewhat interchangeably,
although Nez Perce was the most common usage outside the tribe.

ARTIST'S NOTE

Readers may care to note that the original paintings from which the
color plates in this book were prepared are available for private sale.
The Publishers retain all reproduction copyright whatsoever.
All enquiries should be addressed to:

Peter Dennis, Fieldhead, The Park, Mansfield, NOTTS, NG18 2AT, UK

The Publishers regret that they can enter into no correspondence upon
this matter.

THE WOODLAND TRUST

Osprey Publishing are supporting the Woodland Trust, the UK's leading
woodland conservation charity, by funding the dedication of trees.

Key to military symbols

Army Group	Army
Corps	Division
Brigade	Regiment
Battalion	Company/Battery
Platoon	Section
Squad	Infantry
Artillery	Cavalry
Airborne	Unit HQ
Air defence	Air Force
Air mobile	Air transportable
Amphibious	Anti-tank
Armour	Air aviation
Bridging	Engineer
Headquarters	Maintenance
Medical	Missile
Mountain	Navy
Nuclear, biological, chemical	Ordnance
Parachute	Reconnaissance
Signal	Supply
Transport movement	Rocket artillery
Air defence artillery	

Key to unit identification

Unit identifier / Parent unit / Commander
(+) with added elements
(−) less elements

CONTENTS

Arrival Of The Nez Perce Indians at Walla Walla Treaty May 1855

Arrival of The Nez Perce Indians to the Wallawalla Treaty

ORIGINS OF THE CAMPAIGN

Nature abhors a vacuum
François Rabelais, 1532

Hundreds of years ago, the Nimiipuu tribe settled along the Clearwater River in central Idaho, centered upon a large volcanic mound of rock known as the "Heart of the Monster." Tribal traditions extend back only about three to four centuries, so it is likely that the Nimiipuu had antecedents among other tribes in the Pacific Northwest. Although the core territory held by the Nimiipuu was focused along the Clearwater River, the subsistence economy of the tribe – based on salmon fishing and gathering camas roots on the Weippe Prairie – forced its members to spread out to seek new food resources. Eventually, the Nimiipuu divided into sub-clans that lived in dispersed villages. These sub-clans, numbering at most a few hundred persons each, were semi-nomadic, occupying the lowland prairies in summer and then moving to the high canyons in the fall to avoid the worst of the winter snow. The Nimiipuu were also ethnically related to several nearby tribes, including the Palouse, Cayuse and the Umatilla. By the early 18th century, the Nimiipuu acquired horses from southern tribes, allowing them to send summer expeditions to the Great Plains to hunt buffalo. However, as the tribe grew in size and power, it clashed with the Shoshone tribe to the southeast and the Blackfeet to the north. The Nimiipuu, which means the "real people," could be very arrogant in dealing with outsiders, which won them few allies.

In September 1805, the starving Lewis and Clark Expedition came down the Lolo Trail and encountered the Nimiipuu on the Weippe Prairie near the Clearwater River, which was the first occasion that the tribe met with Americans. Initially the Nez Perce considered killing the members of the expedition but they were dissuaded by a Nez Perce woman named Wat-Ku-ese, who claimed that other Americans had helped her escape from the Blackfeet. The Nimiipuu offered food and hospitality to the strangers because they wanted to acquire rifles, which the Shoshone and Blackfeet already possessed. Both of these enemies had inflicted losses on the Nimiipuu in recent warfare and the tribe viewed trade with the Americans as a necessity. For their part, Lewis and Clark erroneously labeled the tribe as the "Nez Perce" and proceeded upon their way. Within a few years, Canadian, English and American fur traders began following in the wake of Lewis and Clark, and the Nimiipuu were able to acquire flintlocks, which enabled them to fight on equal terms with the Shoshone and the Blackfeet. Soon, the Nimiipuu began a regular trade with the trappers, swapping horses for weapons and gunpowder. With their newfound firepower and mounted on fine horses, the Nimiipuu war chief Broken Arm took 45 scalps from the Shoshone and Chief Red Wolf inflicted heavy losses on the Blackfeet.

5

A row of Nez Perce tepees photographed near the Yellowstone River in 1871. Like most Indian tribes, the Nez Perce preferred a semi-nomadic way of life. However in failing to develop agriculture or construct fixed settlements, the Nez Perce actually made it easier to be dispossessed of their land by others, since they had no tangible signs of ownership. (Library of Congress)

For the first several decades of the 19th century, the Nimiipuu had only limited contact with Americans and it was generally friendly because it suited the tribe's interests. In 1836, a group of American missionaries arrived with a fur caravan and established a school and church on the Clearwater. A number of Nimiipuu converted to Christianity, which began to alter the internal dynamics of the tribe. For decades after Lewis and Clark passed through, the Nimiipuu felt immune in their mountain strongholds to the tide of westward-moving American settlers and even the advent of the Oregon Trail in the 1840s had little immediate influence, since it passed well south of Nimiipuu lands. As long as settlers passed through and did some trading along the way, the Nimiipuu were friendly in contact with Americans. For their part, most Americans regarded the Nez Perce as one of the few friendly tribes in the Pacific Northwest. In November 1847, members of the neighboring Cayuse tribe murdered 14 American missionaries in the Whitman Massacre, which precipitated eight years of sporadic conflict known as the Cayuse War. Rather than supporting their kinsmen, the Nimiipuu remained loyal to the Americans and did not lift a finger to help the Cayuse.

As a result of the lawlessness evidenced by the Whitman Massacre, the Oregon Territory was created and at least part of the Nimiipuu lands fell under the nominal jurisdiction of the US Government. After the Cayuse were finally defeated in 1855, the governor of the Oregon Territory sought to delineate tribal lands from lands open to settlement in order to reduce the risk of further conflict. A great council was called at Mill Creek near Walla Walla in May 1855 to hammer out a series of treaties between Oregon – acting as a proxy for the US Government – and the local tribes. The defeated Cayuse and the restive Umatillas were treated harshly, losing much of their lands and being forced onto small reservations. Although the Nez Perce were enjoined to sign a treaty as well, because of their help in the Cayuse War they were not required to involuntarily relinquish any land, although settlers could purchase land with their consent. The conversion of large numbers of Nez Perce to Christianity also predisposed the governor of Oregon to use the carrot rather than the stick with them, promising cash and trade gifts. Despite the fact that the governor lacked the military power to force Old Joseph, Looking Glass and other Nimiipuu leaders to sign the treaty, they did so anyway. When the dispossessed Cayuse, Yakima and other tribes resisted resettlement and murdered American miners shortly after the treaty was signed, beginning the Yakima War, the Nez Perce again sided with the Americans and provided 30 scouts to the US Army.

The Treaty of 1855 seemed to safeguard Nimiipuu interests but it caused a rift with neighboring tribes who lost land as a result. The Nimiipuu were living well on their own lands, enjoying a profitable trade with American merchants, but their potential allies were defeated piecemeal by American military forces or marginalized on reservations. Gradually, Nez Perce lands were becoming surrounded by American settlements. The Oregon Territory was reorganized with the creation of the Washington Territory in 1853 and then Oregon became a state in 1859. By 1860, there were over 60,000 American settlers bordering the 12,000 square miles (31,000 square kilometers) of territory held by only 3,000 Nez Perce, which created pressure for expansion onto the lands reserved by the Treaty of 1855. Complacent with their gifts and pledges of protection, the Nimiipuu leadership was only vaguely aware that the correlation of forces was shifting against them.

The tipping point came with the discovery of gold in October 1860 at Orofino Creek, on Nez Perce land near the Clearwater River. This discovery sparked a gold rush by thousands of unauthorized miners and in short orders, towns such as Lewiston and Elk City were built illegally on Nez Perce lands. In a matter of months, the newcomers outnumbered the Nimiipuu. The US Army tried to inhibit illegal immigration and built Fort Lapwai on Nez Perce lands with tribal permission in 1862, but the two-company garrison was too small to impede the gold rush. Bowing to the inevitable, local officials called a meeting with Nez Perce leaders at Fort Lapwai in May 1863 to discuss a new treaty. American negotiators claimed that a new treaty was necessary since the reservation granted by the 1855 Treaty was too large to be patrolled by fewer than 200 troops and that a smaller reservation would be easier to protect. After much arm-twisting and promises of more gifts, most of the Christianized Nimiipuu from the northern areas – which were contained within the new boundaries – reluctantly agreed to sign the treaty. However, Old Joseph's group would lose their home in the Wallowa Valley, as would the other southern groups of the Nimiipuu, so they decided to boycott the treaty and walked out without signing. Thus, the 1863 Treaty, which the Nez Perce referred to as the "Steal Treaty," further divided the Nimiipuu into Treaty and Non-Treaty factions.

After leaving the Lapwai council, the minority Non-Treaty factions, numbering less than 1,000 members, returned to their villages and began to reject dealing with the Americans and turned for spiritual comfort to the nascent "Dreamer Movement," a shamanistic cult that preached clinging on to the traditional Nez Perce culture. Many Dreamers also believed that some unknown spiritual force would soon remove settlers from their lands, so it really didn't matter what the Americans said.

OLLOKOT'S AND HOWARD'S ULTIMATUMS

The gold rush along the Clearwater ended with a whimper after just a few years, but American settlers continued to pour into Nez Perce lands. While the Non-Treaty factions ignored the 1863 Treaty, the US Government did not make any effort to force them onto approved reservation lands for more than a decade. In 1871, Old Joseph died and his son Joseph assumed leadership over the Wallowa band – which numbered fewer than 200 souls – just as the first American settlers arrived in the valley. Although adamant about not ceding his father's land, Joseph recognized the futility of provoking armed

Yellow Bull (Chuslum Moxmox), a warchief of the Lamátta band who led the second series of raids along the Salmon River that sparked the Nez Perce War. He played a significant role in the fighting throughout the campaign, surrendered at Bear Paw and would eventually return to the Lapwai Reservation. (Author's collection)

conflict with the Americans and advocated a policy of cooperation with the settlers. When Brigadier-General Oliver Howard took command of the Department of the Columbia in 1874 he looked with sympathy upon the Non-Treaty Nez Perce and recommended letting "these really peaceable Indians… have this poor valley [the Wallowa] for their own." By 1875 there were a few hundred American settlers establishing farms in the valley, but many Nez Perce were incensed when settlers ploughed the land, claiming that it "profaned the Earth Mother." On June 22, 1876, an incident occurred when an American settler killed Wind Blowing (Wilhautyah), a friend of Joseph, during an argument. The Nez Perce claimed it was murder, although the settlers disagreed. Ten weeks after the incident, Joseph's hotheaded younger brother, Ollokot, issued an ultimatum on September 2 that the murderers had to be handed over to the Nez Perce and that all settlers had to leave the Wallowa Valley within one week or suffer the consequences. When the settlers refused and began to assemble a volunteer militia, Ollokot threatened that the Nez Perce would drive them out by force and burn their houses.

Upon hearing about the disturbance, Howard sent a cavalry company to the Wallowa Valley, which arrived just as the militia and Nez Perce were about to come to blows. However, the cavalry lieutenant judiciously hammered out a compromise that defused the crisis. Joseph and Ollokot agreed to drop their ultimatum, as long as the men responsible for the death of Wind Blowing faced trial. Yet the Nez Perce had no faith in the trial and the witnesses they sent refused to testify, so the case was dismissed. Although the crisis appeared to have passed, Howard was resolved to avoid future land disputes with the Non-Treaty Nez Perce and resolved to enforce the 1863 Treaty. Given the recent defeat of Custer at the Little Bighorn, American attitudes were hardening against troublesome Indian tribes and Howard could not allow any more Nez Perce ultimatums to local settlers. He called for a meeting with Joseph and other Non-Treaty Nez Perce leaders at the Lapwai Agency on November 13, 1876, to discuss future relations. Once there, Howard informed them that he regarded them as bound by the 1863 Treaty and that they would have to move to the Lapwai Reservation. Joseph responded that his clan's traditions would not allow him to cede the Wallowa Valley. Howard wasn't prepared for a flat-out refusal, so nothing happened for six months as he dithered about what step to take next.

Figuring that Howard was bound to take action sooner or later, the leaders of the five Non-Treaty bands decided to be proactive by traveling to Fort Lapwai on May 4, 1877, to discuss the situation. There were four Nez Perce bands – the Alpowai, led by Looking Glass; White Bird's group near the Salmon River; Toohoolhoolzote's group near the Snake River; and Joseph's group in the Wallowa Valley – as well as the Palouse tribe, led by Hahtalekin, who were closely related to the Nez Perce. Oddly, the leaders allowed the bellicose Toohoolhoolzote rather than the more diplomatic Joseph to do their talking, which was a huge mistake. Toohoolhoolzote's tirades quickly enraged Howard and obliterated any desire within him to negotiate. Howard then demanded that the Non-Treaty bands move onto the reservation by June 15 or he would use troops to force them, yelling that "You will come on the reservation within the time I tell you. If not, soldiers will put you there or shoot you down!" In the face of Toohoolhoolzote's obstinate refusal, Howard jailed him for a week. Suddenly growing submissive in the face of Howard's threats, Joseph, White Bird and the other leaders, meekly agreed to move onto the Lapwai Reservation. The leaders then returned to gather up their families, cattle and belongings and scheduled a gathering at Tolo Lake south of the reservation for early June.

One unintended consequence of Howard's ultimatum was that it forced the Wallowa band to cross both the Snake and Salmon rivers at flood tide after the spring snow melted. In order to cross the rivers, the Wallowa band constructed Mackinaw boats and floatation devices made from animal skins. The experience the Wallowa band gained crossing the Snake and Salmon rivers just before the war began proved to be a valuable dress rehearsal that would give them a major advantage in evading Howard's troops.

Howard was satisfied that he had resolved the Non-Treaty Nez Perce situation and looked forward to congratulations from Washington, DC, but he had made the mistake of issuing an ultimatum without having sufficient military forces at hand to back it up. Further, he should have dealt with each faction individually, rather than uniting them with a single ultimatum. Howard failed to appreciate the sense of humiliation that he had collectively inflicted on the five Non-Treaty leaders and that he discredited Joseph's policy of cooperation. Clearly, the policy of accommodation had gained the Non-Treaty factions nothing. Even as the groups gathered up their belongings and left their homelands in compliance with Howard's ultimatum, more Nez Perce began to see violence rather than talking as the solution to their problems.

By June 3, about 590 members from the five Non-Treaty bands began to gather near Tolo Lake, where the Nez Perce traditionally held Dreamer rituals in summer, before heading on to the reservation. Since there was still time before Howard's ultimatum expired, many of the Non-Treaty factions decided to savor their last days of freedom and some men indulged in a week-long drinking binge. Any control that the clan chieftains had over their members virtually disintegrated during this period. After a week of grumbling about Howard's ultimatum and drinking, intemperate heads began to make the decisions, not Joseph and the other chiefs. An intoxicated young Nez Perce from the White Bird group named Shore Crossing (Wahlitits), whose father Eagle Robe (Tipyahlanah) had been killed by a miner named Larry Ott two years earlier, decided that this was the moment for revenge. Riding south toward the Salmon River on the morning of June 14 with his friends Red Moccasin Tops (Sarpsis llppilp), and Swan Necklace (Wetyetmas Wahyakt), Shore Crossing sought to kill Ott. Instead, he failed to find Ott but opted to murder one Richard Devine in his bed, along with three other American settlers whom he believed guilty of previously harming local Nez Perce. When they returned to the Tolo Lake encampment, Shore Crossing and his friends incited a frenzy to commit more violence. Yellow Bull (Chuslum Moxmox) gathered up 15 warriors from the White Bird group and they went on a two-day spree of murdering, raping and burning along the Salmon River, which resulted in the deaths of at least 14 more Americans, including two infants. Four women were brutally raped. These Nez Perce raids were among the worst massacres of American settlers in the post-Civil War West and the spark that started the Nez Perce War.

CHRONOLOGY

1805	Lewis and Clark Expedition establishes first contact between Nez Perce and US Government.
1836	First Protestant missionaries arrive among Nez Perce.
1846	Oregon Treaty establishes US jurisdiction over the Pacific Northwest.
1855	Isaac Stevens, Governor of the Oregon Territory, forces the Nez Perce and other tribes to sign treaties that severely limit their tribal lands. As a result, the Nez Perce split into Treaty and Non-Treaty factions.
1860	Gold is discovered on Nez Perce territory, bringing thousands of settlers illegally onto Nez Perce land.
1862	The US Army constructs Fort Lapwai on Nez Perce land to support the Indian Agency.
1863	The US Government forces the Nez Perce to sign a new treaty that reduces their reservation to only 10 percent of the land set aside by the 1855 Treaty.
1871	
January	With The Indian Appropriation Act, the US Congress decides that instead of signing new treaties with Indian tribes as 'independent nations,' the US Government will now dictate tribal reservation areas.
August	When his father dies, Young Joseph becomes chief of his band of the Nez Perce.

1876

June 25	Custer's command is wiped out at the battle of Little Bighorn by the Sioux, Arapaho and Cheyenne.
June 22	A settler kills Wind Blowing, a Nez Perce, sparking a crisis in the Wallowa Valley.
September 8–13	The Wallowa Crisis ends in compromise.
November 13	Brigadier-General Howard meets with Joseph and the Non-Treaty Nez Perce leaders and demands that they move onto the Lapwai reservation.

1877

May 3–14	Howard meets again with the Non-Treaty Nez Perce leaders and demands that they comply with the 1863 treaty by June 15.
June 3	The five Non-Treaty bands converge on Tolo Lake, prior to heading to Lapwai.
June 14	A small number of Nez Perce warriors go on a rampage along the Salmon River, killing 18 American civilians.
June 15	Howard receives word of the attacks and dispatches two cavalry troops under Captain Perry to protect civilians around Grangeville.
June 16	Perry arrives in Grangeville, where the civilians prevail upon him to punish the Nez Perce before they can flee.
June 17	Perry's command is defeated at the battle of White Bird Canyon.
June 23	Howard marches out of Fort Lapwai with a column to pursue the Nez Perce.
June 29	Howard orders a pre-emptive strike on the camp of Chief Looking Glass, even though his faction is still on reservation land.
June 30	As Howard crosses the Salmon River, the Nez Perce slip away and cross to the opposite side at Craig's Ferry.
July 1	Captain Stephen G. Whipple conducts a morning raid on Looking Glass's camp.
July 2	Howard orders Whipple to defend the Cottonwood ranch and to determine where the Nez Perce are heading after crossing the Salmon.
July 3	Whipple's scouts spot the Nez Perce, but they in turn annihilate Second Lieutenant Sevier M. Rains's detachment.

July 4–5	The Nez Perce attack Whipple's command at the Cottonwood.
July 7	The Nez Perce establish a new camp on the Clearwater River and link up with Looking Glass's faction.
July 8	Colonel McConville's volunteers discover the Nez Perce village and send word to Howard.
July 9	Howard moves out of Grangeville and advances toward the Clearwater. McConville's force is besieged on "Misery Hill."
July 11–12	Howard's forces attack the Nez Perce village in the indecisive battle of the Clearwater.
July 16	The Nez Perce begin moving up the Lolo Trail to Montana.
July 22	The Nez Perce reach Lolo Pass.
July 28	The Nez Perce bypass the blocking position dubbed "Fort Fizzle."
August 4	Colonel Gibbon begins a pursuit down the Bitterroot Valley.
August 7	Army scouts discover the Nez Perce village at the Big Hole.
August 9	Colonel Gibbon's column attacks the Nez Perce village in the sanguinary battle of the Big Hole.
August 12	Colonel Miles sends Colonel Sturgis and part of the 7th Cavalry to prevent the Nez Perce from reaching the plains of Montana.
August 13	The Nez Perce cross the Bannock Pass back into Idaho.
August 20	The Nez Perce conduct a mounted raid against Howard's camp at Camas Meadows.
August 23	The Nez Perce cross the Targhee Pass into Yellowstone National Park.
September 5	Sturgis reaches Clark's Fork of the Yellowstone River and awaits the Nez Perce.
September 8	The Nez Perce spot Sturgis and conduct a feint that causes him to leave Clark's Fork unguarded.
September 9	The Nez Perce slip through Clark's Fork, reaching the flatlands.
September 11	Sturgis and Howard link up near Clark's Fork. Howard orders Sturgis to force-march after the Nez Perce.
September 12	The Nez Perce cross the Yellowstone River.

September 13	Sturgis skirmishes with the Nez Perce at Canyon Creek but fails to halt them.
September 18	Miles moves out of the Tongue River cantonment to intercept the Nez Perce.
September 23–24	The Nez Perce attack the supply depot at Cow Island on the Missouri River.
September 30	Miles finds and attacks the Nez Perce near Bear Paw Mountain. After initial attacks are repulsed, Miles settles in for a siege.
October 1	Miles violates a truce and captures Joseph but is later forced to exchange him for a captured officer.
October 3–4	Miles bombards the trapped Nez Perce.
October 5	Joseph and 418 Nez Perce surrender.
1878	Nez Perce prisoners are deported to the Indian Territory.
1881	Last Nez Perce refugees return from Canada.
1883–85	Most Nez Perce are returned to either the Lapwai or Colville reservations.

OPPOSING COMMANDERS

Brigadier-General Oliver Howard, as he appeared during the Civil War. Howard failed to appreciate that the clumsy and firepower-intensive methods of the Civil War were ill suited to Indian warfare and his inability to suppress the Nez Perce uprising quickly encouraged other local tribes to go on the warpath in the following year. (Library of Congress)

US ARMY

The American commanders who fought in the Nez Perce Campaign were all veterans of the Civil War and their experience in that conflict shaped their methods of warfare. Each had risen to at least division command during that conflict and demonstrated competence in maneuvering troops in the field. Except for Howard, all had prior experience in the peculiar requirements of Indian fighting. Although General William T. Sherman, commanding general of the US Army, made a number of statements in 1866–69 about exterminating hostile Indian tribes, the commanders who fought the Nez Perce did not believe or practice genocidal methods. Rather, the army leaders who fought the Nez Perce were driven by personal agendas, ranging from desire for promotion to avoiding the appearance of failure.

Brigadier-General Oliver O. Howard (1830–1909)

Howard had been in command of the Department of the Columbia since July 1874. He was born in Maine and graduated fourth in his class from West Point in 1854. Commissioned as a second lieutenant in the ordnance branch, Howard served in non-troop assignments for the first seven years of his career, including instructing mathematics at West Point. In 1857, he converted to Evangelical Christianity, which had a profound effect upon his later attitudes and his relationship with his fellow soldiers and the Nez Perce. He tended to select and favor officers whom he considered "active Christians" while despising those Indians who rejected Christianity.

At the start of the Civil War, Howard was made a brevet colonel and served as a brigade commander at the battle of First Manassas and during the Peninsula Campaign. At the battle of Fair Oaks on June 1, 1862, Howard was shot twice while leading his brigade, requiring the amputation of his right arm. Over 30 years later, Howard was awarded the Medal of Honor for this action. After a very brief recovery, he returned to the Army of the Potomac and took over the Second Division in II Corps when Major-General John Sedgwick was wounded at the battle of Antietam. At both Antietam and Fredericksburg, Howard led his division in costly and futile frontal assaults that were repulsed. Shortly afterwards, Howard was promoted to major-general and given command of XI Corps. On May 2, 1863, Howard's corps was routed at the battle of Chancellorsville when struck in a surprise attack by Stonewall Jackson's forces after Howard had disregarded the enemy's ability to maneuver through heavily wooded terrain and had failed to take adequate security precautions. On July 1, 1863, Howard's corps was again routed on the first day of the battle of Gettysburg and suffered 41 percent casualties. Arguably the most important moment in Howard's military career came when he made the spot decision to anchor the Union "fishhook" defensive position on Cemetery Hill – a position that he successfully defended for the next two days. After Gettysburg, Howard's corps was transferred west to the Army of the Cumberland and he fought in the battle of Chattanooga. During the Atlanta Campaign, he badly fumbled a flank attack at Pickett's Mill on May 27, 1864, and then failed to sever the last Confederate-held rail line into Atlanta. Despite this lackluster performance, Howard was given command of the Army of Tennessee in July 1864, which he commanded during Sherman's March to the Sea and subsequent campaign in the Carolinas. Howard gained considerable experience with handling large formations during the Civil War but his combat record was primarily of failure. Formations under his command tended to achieve little while suffering heavy losses. Combined with this his intolerance to drinking and swearing, Howard inspired little confidence in his troops.

Colonel John Gibbon, commander of the 7th Infantry, succeeded in surprising the Nez Perce at the Big Hole but nearly lost his command in the process. Gibbon was also intimately familiar with the terrain in Yellowstone National Park but he was *hors de combat* by the time that the Nez Perce reached the park after the battle of the Big Hole. (Library of Congress)

After the war ended, Howard was appointed commissioner of the Freedman's Bureau, more for his missionary zeal than his organizational talents. Howard spent the next seven years knee-deep in Reconstruction issues but far removed from any military duties. In mid-1872, Howard was sent to Arizona to negotiate with the Chiricahua Apaches and he successfully forged a peace treaty with Cochise. Nevertheless, Howard's military career might have been over had not the Modoc Indians murdered Major-General Edward Canby, the head of the Department of the Columbia in April 1873. Since the postwar US Army had few other generals lying around unemployed and Howard appeared well suited to the job of reining in the Non-Treaty Nez Perce, he was sent west as a negotiator, not as a combat commander. Howard was a world-class military incompetent, often inclined to lie or shift blame about his failures. There is no doubt that Howard was intelligent and perhaps a bit of an intellectual, but he was not inclined to make decisions quickly or to accept advice easily from others. His style of command was probably best suited to static positional warfare, but he had no head for a war of maneuver. He consistently failed to understand either the terrain or the enemy and drove his long-suffering troops as if they were a pack of mules.

Colonel John Gibbon (1827–96)

Born in Philadelphia but raised in North Carolina, John Gibbon graduated from West Point in 1847 and was commissioned in the artillery. He saw no combat in the Mexican War but served in Florida against the Seminoles. Just before the Civil War, he was teaching artillery tactics at West Point. During the Civil War, Gibbon was promoted to brigadier-general of volunteers in May 1862 and successfully led the Iron Brigade at Second Manassas, South Mountain and Antietam. At Brawner's Farm on August 28, 1862, Gibbon's brigade stubbornly held off a surprise flank attack by Stonewall Jackson's Corps, despite being outnumbered three to one. Afterwards, Gibbon was elevated to division command and held this role for the next two years through some of the thickest fighting of the Civil War. He spent much of the war serving under the best corps commanders that the Union Army had to offer – John Reynolds and Winfield Hancock. On the third day at Gettysburg, Gibbon's division helped to defeat Longstreet's assault, although Gibbon was

Colonel Samuel D. Sturgis, commander of the 7th Cavalry. Sturgis was brilliantly outmaneuvered at Clark's Fork Canyon and then tried to atone by riding his cavalry until a third of his horses died, leaving his command immobilized. (Library of Congress)

wounded. Later, he returned to command his division during the battles of the Wilderness, Spotsylvania and Cold Harbor. In January 1865 Major-General Gibbon took command of XXIV Corps, which he led successfully during the Petersburg and Appomattox campaigns. By the end of the war, Gibbon had gained an immense amount of combat experience and had repeatedly demonstrated battlefield competence.

Reverting to colonel in the regular army after the war, Gibbon helped to explore Yellowstone National Park. During the Sioux Campaign of 1876, he led the Montana column and was the first to reach Major Reno's surviving remnants of the 7th Cavalry. At the start of the Nez Perce War in June 1877, Gibbon was commander of Fort Ellis near Bozeman, Montana and responsible for the western part of the territory. Gibbon was tough, experienced and aggressive but he was handicapped by inadequate resources and must have resented serving under a less capable senior officer, such as Howard.

Colonel Samuel D. Sturgis (1822–99)

Commander of the 7th Cavalry since May 1869. Sturgis was born in Pennsylvania and graduated from West Point in 1846, where he was commissioned in the dragoons. Just prior to the battle of Buena Vista in February 1847, Sturgis was captured by the Mexicans while on a reconnaissance patrol, but was released after barely a week in captivity. After the Mexican War, Sturgis earned his spurs with the 1st US Dragoons, fighting the Apaches in Texas and New Mexico. In January 1855, Lieutenant Sturgis tracked down and defeated a raiding party of Mescalero Apaches after a 175-mile (280km) pursuit. In 1860, Sturgis successfully intercepted a Kiowa raiding group in Kansas.

Although he was only a captain at the start of the Civil War, Sturgis was an experienced cavalry officer and he was promoted to major and given a brigade in Brigadier-General Nathaniel Lyon's Army of the West. When Lyon was killed at the battle of Wilson's Creek in Missouri on August 10, 1861, Sturgis took command at a critical moment and conducted an orderly withdrawal. Having demonstrated battlefield competence, Sturgis was appointed brigadier-general of volunteers in 1862 and given command of the 2nd Division, IX Corps. He performed well at South Mountain and his division captured Burnside's Bridge at the battle of Antietam, but at Fredericksburg his division suffered 21 percent casualties in the futile assault upon Marye's Heights. After Fredericksburg, Sturgis was relieved of command and sent to Tennessee for occupation duties. In June 1864, Sherman ordered him to deal with Major-General Nathan Bedford Forrest's cavalry raids on Union lines of communication but Forrest decisively defeated Sturgis at the battle of Brice's Crossroads. Despite a five-to-two numerical superiority, Sturgis's command was smashed and Forrest captured 1,500 of his men and 16 guns. Sturgis was relieved again.

After the Civil War ended, Sturgis reverted to the rank of lieutenant-colonel in the regular army and was given command of the 7th Cavalry. He missed the Sioux campaign of 1876 but his son was killed with Custer's battalion at Little Bighorn. Sturgis was a very experienced cavalryman and Indian fighter, but no longer had the self-confidence required for independent command.

Colonel Nelson A. Miles (1839–1925)

Unlike the other army commanders in the Nez Perce War, Miles had not attended West Point. Instead, he was a self-taught civilian with an enthusiasm for military affairs who was working as a clerk in his uncle's store in Boston at the start of the Civil War. Miles managed to borrow $3,000, which he used to organize a company for the 22nd Massachusetts Volunteers and he was appointed as a second lieutenant. In November 1861, Miles was assigned as aide to Oliver Howard and served under him in the Peninsula campaign. When Howard was wounded at Seven Pines, Miles held the shattered arm as it was being amputated.

Miles was intensely ambitious and he was able to gain promotion and command of the 61st New York Volunteers, which he ably led at Antietam, Fredericksburg and Chancellorsville. Miles was badly wounded at the last action, for which he was awarded the Medal of Honor and gained the admiration of his corps commander, Winfield Hancock. Although his recovery was slow, Miles was given command of a division under Hancock in 1863 and he demonstrated innate aggressiveness in fierce attacks at Spotsylvania Court House, Cold Harbor and Petersburg. Thanks to his superb battlefield performance and the support of senior officers such as Howard and Hancock, Miles was breveted a brigadier at age 26 and ended the war as a major-general of volunteers.

Colonel Nelson "Bear Coat" Miles, commander of the 5th Infantry in 1877 and one of the most dynamic soldiers in the US Army of the mid-19th century. He was a self-made man and blatantly ambitious, which caused friction with his less-capable peers and superiors, but nobody was better at running hostile Indian groups to ground than Miles. His aggressive use of infantry in winter campaigning over rough terrain set a standard that has never been bettered by other American troops. Miles's victory at Bear Paw salvaged the reputation of the US Army in an otherwise mismanaged campaign. (Author's collection)

After the Civil War, Miles was given command of Fort Monroe and served as jailor of Jefferson Davis, the former Confederate President. He also managed to finesse the rank of colonel in the regular army and married the niece of General William T. Sherman. He spent two years in North Carolina on Reconstruction duty, working closely with Howard's Freedman's Bureau, then was sent west to take over the 5th Infantry in 1869. Miles successfully led a column against the Comanches and Kiowas in the Red River War of 1874 in Texas and Oklahoma. He was a close friend of George Custer and after the Little Bighorn defeat in June 1876, Miles led 400 infantrymen of the 5th Infantry in a series of grueling winter campaigns that harried Sitting Bull into Canada and defeated Crazy Horse at the battle of Wolf Mountains in January 1877. Unlike other officers, Miles did not go into winter quarters but continued to chip away at the hostile tribes, even in sub-zero weather, which earned him the sobriquet "bear coat" for his thick fur garments. Although something of a martinet with his 5th Infantry, Miles was respected by his troops since he insured that they were properly equipped for winter campaigning. Like most army officers of the period, Miles viewed most Indians in negative terms but respected their fighting abilities, commenting that, "the art of war among the white people is called strategy or tactics; when practiced by the Indians it is called treachery."

At the beginning of the Nez Perce Campaign, Miles was in the Tongue River Cantonment in eastern Montana, conducting mop-up operations against the Cheyenne. Miles looked forward to a new campaign as an opportunity to gain promotion to brigadier-general in the regulars. His relationship with Howard was excellent at the start of the campaign but later soured after Bear Paw Mountain. Nelson Miles was probably one of the most energetic, aggressive and experienced brigade-level commanders in the US Army of 1877 and one of the few who had the skill to conduct the kind of high-intensity maneuver warfare that could grind down Indian tribes' ability to remain at large.

NEZ PERCE

As the Non-Treaty Nez Perce were a loose association of five independent bands, they did not have a fixed or unified leadership structure, beyond the basic fact that each faction had a chief. In the Nez Perce, leaders led by

Looking Glass, leader of the Alpowai band and perhaps the most influential of the Nez Perce war chiefs. Although a gifted tactician, Looking Glass's failure to understand the 'big picture' led to catastrophic losses at the Big Hole and Bear Paw. (Author's collection)

Ollokot (center) and two other Nez Perce photographed shortly before the outbreak of war. Ollokot was Joseph's younger brother and war leader of the Wallowa band's 55 warriors. It was Ollokot's ultimatum to the American settlers in the Wallowa Valley that set in motion the events that led to the outbreak of war. (Library of Congress)

consensus rather than diktat. Unlike their opponents, military authority within the Nez Perce was dispersed and non-hierarchical; warriors followed those men they respected and this could change from day to day. One of the great misconceptions about the Nez Perce campaign is that Chief Joseph was a military leader and that he was in charge of all the factions. In fact, he spoke only for his own Wallowa band and he delegated battlefield leadership to his younger, more aggressive brother Ollokot.

Looking Glass (Allalimya Takanin, 1832–77)
The 45-year-old leader of the Alpowai bands, who lived along the Clearwater River. He made a number of trips to Montana on Buffalo hunts and made friends with the local Crow tribe. In 1874, he fought with the Crows against the Sioux along the Yellowstone River and won great prestige. At the beginning of the war, Looking Glass and his band were already located on reservation land in compliance with Howard's ultimatum. Even though Looking Glass tried to dissociate his band from the murders caused by White Bird's band, his group was attacked nonetheless because they were perceived as sympathetic to the hostiles. Looking Glass was in the prime of his life as a warrior and well respected throughout the five factions. He exerted considerable influence both on the overall course of action chosen by the Non-Treaty factions as well as their battlefield tactics, but his authority was never absolute and was actively challenged after he was proven wrong about the supposed sanctuary at the Big Hole. Based upon his prewar experience in Montana, Looking Glass believed that the best option was to seek help with his friends in the Crow tribe, but this also proved illusory. Finally accepting Canada as the only remaining hope, it was Looking Glass who made the fateful decision to rest at Bear Paw rather than push on directly to the border.

Ollokot (1841–77)
Joseph's younger brother and the primary battlefield leader of the Wallowa band, Ollokot had helped to incite the crisis in the Wallowa Valley in the summer of 1876 that eventually led to Howard's ultimatum and he appears to have been more hotheaded than his older brother. On the battlefield, Ollokot was a bold and tough opponent, but apparently lacked the experience to take a larger role in directing the movements of the tribe as a whole. He proved adept at mounted attacks both at White Bird Canyon and Camas Meadows and also played a major role in rearguard actions to delay Howard's pursuit.

Joseph the Younger (Hinmuuttu-yalatlat, 1840–1904)
Chief of the Wallowa band of the Nez Perce. Despite his postwar fame, Joseph did not play a major role in tactical operations during the Nez Perce campaign and served more in administrative and diplomatic roles; it was Joseph who attended to the myriad needs of over 700 people involved in a 1,100-mile (1,770km) march. Initially, Joseph commanded considerable respect among all five Non-Treaty factions and his proposals to seek sanctuary at White Bird Canyon and then evade Howard's pursuit were generally accepted. However unlike most of the other faction leaders, who realized after the battle of White Bird Canyon that they must flee Idaho, Joseph held out for returning to the Wallowa Valley as soon as possible. It was only after crossing into Montana that Joseph began to realize that there was no going back and his opinions carried less weight than those proposing

escape to Canada. After defeat at Bear Paw, Joseph spent the rest of his life telling the American press how his people had been wronged, while glossing over the fact that they had started the war and murdered dozens of American civilians.

White Bird (Peo-peo-hix-hiix, 18??–92)

Leader of the Lamátta band of the Nez Perce. Like the other Non-Treaty faction leaders, White Bird adhered to the Dreamer movement and adopted hard-line, traditionalist attitudes. Of all the Nez Perce leaders, he was the most hostile to Americans and notions of mutual coexistence. It was members of his group who played a leading role in the incidents that led to the outbreak of war. Initially, White Bird was the senior war chief of the Non-Treaty factions, but gradually lost his authority to Looking Glass, who was a better tactician. After the battle of Bear Paw, White Bird evaded Miles's troops and escaped to Canada with some of his band. He lived in Alberta for the next 15 years until one of his followers, angry about their poor living conditions, murdered him with an axe.

Joseph, Chief of the Wallowa band in 1877. For over a century, Joseph has been mistakenly labeled as the military leader of the entire Non-Treaty Nez Perce faction and as the "Red Napoleon" by an ignorant Eastern press establishment. In fact, Joseph was more of a steward, attending to the daily needs of a people in flight and left battlefield command to others. Postwar accounts inflated Joseph's role since most of the actual war chiefs were either dead or in Canada and he became lionized as a "hero," rather than a delusional nonconformist who led his people to defeat and exile. (Author's collection)

Toohoolhoolzote (182?–77)

Leader of one of the Pikunan band that lived along the Snake River. Toohoolhoolzote was adamantly opposed to moving onto the reservation or abandoning his Dreamer ways in favor of farming. He played a major, if pugnacious role, in prewar negotiations and his arrest by Howard contributed to the breakdown in relations. Indeed, Toohoolhoolzote's anti-Christian remarks brought out the worst in Howard. Although over 50, Toohoolhoolzote was an active war chief and played a major role in the battle of the Clearwater. He was caught in the open by US cavalry at the battle of Bear Paw and killed.

Red Echo (Hahtalekin, 1843–77)

Chief of the small Palouse band, which was the only other Indian faction allied with the Non-Treaty Nez Perce. Hahtalekin and his son were both killed at the Big Hole.

Poker Joe/Lean Elk/Hototo (18??–77)

A half-breed Nez Perce, part French, who became de facto trail leader of the Non-Treaty factions in the Bitterroot Valley of Montana and then through the Yellowstone National Park. Poker Joe was in Montana at the start of the war and he joined the Non-Treaty factions just before the Big Hole. His local knowledge was invaluable during the period from the Big Hole to the crossing of the Yellowstone but after that, he yielded to Looking Glass's leadership. At the battle of Bear Paw, he was mistaken for a Cheyenne scout and accidently shot by a fellow Nez Perce.

OPPOSING FORCES

US ARMY

The US Army committed about 1,800 troops during the three-month-long Nez Perce campaign, although no more than 520 were ever actively engaged at one time against the Nez Perce. While the US Army enjoyed an average battlefield numerical superiority of two to one or better against the Nez Perce, it proved difficult to use this factor to their advantage against a fleeting opponent. The army demonstrated repeated difficulty in crossing rivers that the enemy – encumbered with women and children – could cross with relative ease. Compounding this, most units in the US Army lacked the kind of tactical agility required to run a clever enemy like the Nez Perce to ground and relied almost entirely upon superior numbers to carry the day. Given that Howard's forces represented the pointy end of the spear of an industrial-era army fighting a campaign against essentially a Stone Age tribe, this dependence upon quantity demonstrates the doctrinal poverty of the army's leadership.

A group of soldiers in the mid-1870s. Because of the low pay and social status of many soldiers, the American public and media disdained regular troops and the US Army was forced to fight a series of counter-insurgency campaigns on the frontier without the benefit of public support. Much of the later sympathy for the defeated Nez Perce arose from widespread disinformation from Eastern newspapers, who never bothered to interview lowly soldiers such as these. Instead, the Eastern press often depicted the frontier soldiers as "savages," while ignoring the atrocities committed by Indians. (Author's collection)

LEFT
Troops of the 1st US Cavalry in garrison. Many of the troops assigned to Howard's command came from quiet posts in Oregon, Washington and northern California and were not accustomed to hard campaigning. (US Cavalry Museum)

BOTTOM
Company L of the 1st Cavalry assembled in columns of four in garrison. Note the lack of field gear and the presence of three dogs in the formation. In some cavalry units, training consisted of little more than parade ground drills, which explains why the 1st Cavalry proved so poor at reconnaissance and movement to contact in the Nez Perce War. (US Cavalry Museum)

The main units deployed against the Nez Perce were elements of the 1st, 2nd and 7th Cavalry, the 5th, 7th and 21st Infantry and the 4th Artillery. Detachments from each regiment were combined into mixed field forces, subdivided into ad hoc pure cavalry and infantry battalions. The units in Howard's Department of the Columbia had less combat experience than the units stationed in Montana, all of which had participated in the Sioux War of 1876. The 1st Cavalry was particularly mediocre and performed poorly on the battlefield and its small-unit leadership proved timid. In an era when the US Army was particularly poor at reconnaissance, the 1st Cavalry repeatedly lost contact with the Nez Perce and totally failed to keep Howard informed of enemy movements. Both the 2nd and 7th Cavalry had plenty of combat experience but the latter was plagued by the memory of Little Bighorn, which affected its performance. The infantry units possessed greater firepower than the cavalry and were capable of marching 20 miles (32km) per day. Rounding out Howard's force was the 4th Artillery, which primarily served as dismounted infantry. The 4th Artillery was drawn from barracks in Alaska, California and

Oregon and had seen considerable field service in the Modoc and Sioux wars, but the troops were not accustomed to long marches. Typical company field strengths were 50 for cavalry, 25–30 for the infantry and 20–25 for the artillery.

Available data suggests that most of the troops were fairly old, with many in their 30s and 40s. In the 7th Infantry, 37 percent of the troops were foreign born, mostly from Germany and Ireland, including some of the officers. Almost all the troops were northerners, with only a handful of southerners in ranks. Virtually all of the officers above second lieutenant were Civil War veterans and that conflict made an indelible mark upon their understanding of warfare. The better officers learned to adapt to the different conditions of Indian warfare, while the less imaginative ones acted as if they were still fighting the Army of Northern Virginia. Nowhere was this more apparent than the failure of Howard and Gibbon to realize that the Nez Perce pony herd was their center of gravity and that, if deprived of it, their ability to evade pursuit would be severely degraded.

Army doctrine at this time emphasized the use of converging columns to corner and destroy a fleeing Indian force, but this proved exceedingly difficult during the Nez Perce campaign owing to the rugged nature of the terrain and the difficulty of coordination between dispersed field columns. Despite the availability of telegraph that allowed Howard and Terry to coordinate at the operational level, tactical coordination still relied on mounted couriers, who proved exceedingly vulnerable to enemy interception or simply getting lost. Consequently, the Nez Perce never had to fight more than one pursuing column at a time. If the enemy could be fixed in place and forced to fight, army tactics sought to use linear skirmish lines to mass firepower in order to create a "kill zone" to their front. Breech-loading small arms, combined with artillery and Gatling guns, seemed to offer a huge advantage in firepower over less well-armed Indian warriors. This tactic worked fairly well against linear opponents in the Civil War, but it proved too inflexible against the non-linear fighting methods of tribes such as the Nez Perce. Rather than walking dumbly in large, concentrated formations into the army's firepower buzz saw, the Nez Perce fought in small, very mobile groups of warriors that hugged the flanks of the linear army formations and avoided their teeth. Most ammunition fired by the US Army in the Nez Perce campaign literally hit air, unable to strike the elusive foe.

In theory, the firepower of US Army units was formidable. The infantry had received the Model 1873 Trapdoor Springfield breech-loading rifle in the summer of 1874, which could accurately fire a .45/70 caliber (11.6mm) bullet out to 600 yards (550m). The cavalry's Springfield carbines had less range but were still quite effective within 300 yards (225m). Even with the small companies of 1877, the US Army could still pour over 250 rounds per minute into the kill zone in front of a typical skirmish line. However, owing to the cost of ammunition target practice with the new breech-loaders was limited to as few as 20 rounds per year. As Second Lieutenant Harry L. Bailey, from Company B, 21st Infantry, noted, "we had almost no target practice" on account of tight budgets and the troops fired only short distances and often too high. At the battle of the Rosebud on June 17, 1876, Brigadier-General Crook's 15 companies of the 2nd and 3rd Cavalry fired about 80,000 rounds, which caused only 31 Indian casualties – indicating an average of more than 2,500 rounds fired to inflict a single casualty. After the defeat at Little Bighorn, the US Army decided to increase marksmanship training, but the impact on the forces deployed in the Nez Perce campaign appear to have been negligible. At the Big Hole, soldiers fired repeatedly at opponents who were within 50 yards (45m) and missed. Anecdotal evidence suggests that most Indian casualties occurred from point-blank pistol fire, and that the dreaded firepower of US Army skirmish lines produced little more than smoke and noise.

Sticking to the Civil War tradition of more firepower is best, the US Army leadership tried to compensate for the small size of its field forces by adding Gatling guns and howitzers, although some commanders were dubious about their value in Indian warfare. The ten-barreled, hand-cranked improved Gatling gun introduced in 1871 could fire 350 .50/70-caliber rounds per minute, which gave firepower equivalent to an infantry company. It was used in combat against Indians for the first time by Colonel Nelson A. Miles during the Red River War of 1874–75 but Miles had a low opinion of the weapon, reporting that, "they are worthless for Indian fighting. The range is no longer than the rifle and the bullets so small that you cannot tell where they strike." Furthermore, the models available in 1877 were mounted on heavy artillery caissons that made them difficult to maneuver or employ on the roadless terrain on the frontier. When Gatling guns were used against the Nez Perce, they forced the enemy to keep their distance but inflicted negligible damage. Slightly more useful were a small number of mountain howitzers that could be broken down into several loads and transported on mules. Unlike cannons, the howitzers could lob explosive shells into dead space where Indians were lurking to avoid direct fire. The standard 12-pdr howitzer was used with mixed results throughout the Nez Perce campaign, partly because commanders tended to deploy it too far from intended targets. The army had just purchased a few 1.65in. mountain guns from the French firm of Hotchkiss and these weapons saw their first service at the battle of Bear Paw.

Logistical support for mobile field forces proved difficult during the Nez Perce campaign, owing to the lack of roads or railroads and the distances involved. Each column had to be accompanied by several dozen wagons, which could carry enough provisions for only 10–15 days. Furthermore, logistics were dependent upon hiring civilian teamsters and their availability often inflicted operational delays upon the pursuit of the Nez Perce. Howard's pursuit was hamstrung by inadequate supply operations from the beginning, ranging from lack of food and tents to boats for river crossing. In the event of a drawn-out battle, like the Clearwater, most of the column's ammunition could be consumed in a single day.

A striking difference between the opposing forces that had great influence upon pursuit operations was their respective ability to cross rivers. While the Nez Perce were able to cross rivers with women and children with relative ease, the US Army of 1877 seemed perplexed whenever confronted by a water obstacle. Although both the Salmon and Clearwater rivers were at flood height in mid-June 1877, neither was more than 110 yards (100m) wide or more than 7–13ft (2–4m) deep where Howard chose to cross, yet each crossing operation consumed a day or more. Part of this was due to Howard's failure to arrange properly for canvas boats, lumber for rafts and ropes, but it is also apparent that most of the units involved were untrained in tactical river crossing and ill prepared to adapt. Although the Pacific Northwest was replete with unbridged rivers, the US Army neither trained extensively on river crossing nor provided sufficient engineer officers to accompany field columns engaged in mobile operations.

As for battlefield intelligence, the army units were highly dependent upon Indian scouts and armed civilian volunteers, both of whom proved tricky to use. Howard used a combination of friendly Nez Perce and Bannock scouts, while Miles relied on Cheyenne and Crow scouts. The use of Indian scouts was an ad hoc measure with most hired only for a single campaign, so they brought local knowledge but little experience in gaining useful information for the US Army. Unless a tight rein was kept on the Indian scouts, they tended to focus more on stealing horses from the Nez Perce pony herd than reporting on enemy movements. Civilian volunteers proved aggressive in Idaho but mostly passive in Montana, based upon local agendas. During the campaign, there were several stretches of a week or more when the army simply did not know where the Nez Perce were, owing to the weaknesses of their reconnaissance methods.

NEZ PERCE

The Nez Perce had a maximum field strength of 225 warriors, if one included every able-bodied male from 16 to 60 years. Of these warriors, about 42 were considered veteran fighters, with experience either in the Yakima War or against the Blackfeet, Shoshone and Sioux. Based upon testimony from Nez Perce survivors, it appears that most of the actual fighting value of the tribe was in these few dozen warriors, who were equipped with the best weapons and knew how to use them. There were five individual bands within the Nez Perce column, which tended to fight under their own leaders, so there was no overall battlefield commander. Nor was there any fixed tactical organization or doctrine within the Nez Perce, so battlefield leadership went to whoever felt particularly bold that day, with little regard for status or age. Warriors could also leave the battlefield whenever they felt, which made it difficult to fight protracted actions. This lack of unity of command and discipline were severe detriments for the Nez Perce, since it made it difficult to form complex battle plans or to mass their forces against enemy weaknesses. In truth, the Nez Perce fought at a decentralized, tactical level – not unlike a modern insurgent force – which greatly limited their options.

An interesting question, rarely if ever asked in histories of the Indian Wars, is what constituted a "warrior." Not every able-bodied Nez Perce male fought and even Joseph was apparently only involved in combat when he had no choice – at the Big Hole. The Nez Perce later made charges that the US Army

A .44-cal. Henry repeating rifle, which had a 16-round magazine and nearly triple the rate of fire of the Springfield. Although rare among Indian warriors, the US Army was concerned about the sale of repeating rifles to Indian tribes on the Great Plains and Pacific Northwest since it outclassed the Springfield breech-loaders in a close-quarter battle. However, the weapon required special ammunition that would have been difficult for the Nez Perce to obtain. (National Museum of American History, Smithsonian Institution)

killed Indian noncombatants, but by their own testimony, males as young as ten and as old as 60 participated in combat. At the battle of the Big Hole, Captain William Logan was probably shot and killed by a Nez Perce woman. Since the Nez Perce all clustered together, with warriors and noncombatants intermixed, the US Army was hard pressed to distinguish armed opponents from noncombatants.

Since the Nez Perce were traditionally a horse-based society, they preferred to fight mounted, but they were also very adept at fighting on foot in mountainous terrain. On foot, they generally operated in loose gaggles of four to five warriors, using cover and concealment to approach their enemies. Unlike other Indian tribes that tended to run away from the US Army's firepower, the Nez Perce were contemptuous of Howard's linear tactics and the faulty marksmanship of his troops and demonstrated an unusual willingness to engage in close combat. Some of the younger warriors taunted Howard's troops with red blankets, trying to attract fire upon themselves and knowing when they emerged unscathed that it would make the soldier's marksmanship seem pathetic. Although the Nez Perce could dig rifle pits and erect stone fieldworks, their methods were offensive-oriented and they made efforts to annihilate isolated army units – as happened to the detachments of lieutenants Theller and Rains.

Initially, the weaponry available to the Nez Perce was a mixed bag, ranging from modern repeaters like the .44-cal. Henry and Winchester rifles and Sharps .50-cal. rifle, to older muzzle-loading rifles, muskets and pistols. After the victory at White Bird Canyon, the Nez Perce acquired 63 Springfield carbines from the 1st Cavalry. Data from US Army casualties indicates that about 25 percent of the injuries came from older muzzle-loaders. Most Nez Perce had at least one firearm, but some were more comfortable with using the traditional bow and arrow. Yellow Wolf commented that one of the Palouse warriors, Five Fogs, used only a hunting bow because "he did not understand the gun." Nez Perce marksmanship among their veteran warriors proved superb – certainly much better than the standard for the Sioux – and they were regularly capable of hitting targets at 300 yards (275m), whereas the soldiers had very limited chance of hitting them at this range. Analysis of the wounds inflicted upon US soldiers during the campaign indicates that approximately 35 percent of all hits scored by Nez Perce marksmen were on the head or torso region, compared with only 16 percent of hits achieved by soldiers. In other words, Nez Perce marksmen were twice as likely to score lethal hits on their adversaries. Late in the campaign, the Nez Perce were running very short of ammunition after crossing the Yellowstone River and this reduced their ability to fight protracted battles.

Throughout the campaign, the Nez Perce demonstrated an unwillingness to take prisoners unless they were useful and a wanton disregard when it came to targeting local civilians who crossed their path. Unlike the romantic tribe later dreamed up by the Eastern press, the Nez Perce of 1877 were a savage and arrogant foe who could have spared defeated enemies or civilians, but chose to forego mercy. There is no record that Joseph or any of the other tribal leadership ever chastised warriors for murdering or raping civilians, or exterminating trapped foes to the last man – in the Nez Perce lexicon these were acceptable forms of warfare, as long as they were waged on their enemy.

ORDERS OF BATTLE

US ARMY

BATTLE OF WHITE BIRD CANYON, JUNE 17, 1877

1st Cavalry (Companies F, H) (Captain David Perry)
Civilian volunteers (11)
Total: 103 soldiers and 11 civilians

BATTLE OF THE CLEARWATER, JULY 11, 1877

Brigadier-General Oliver O. Howard
1st Cavalry (Companies E, F, H, L, M) (Captain David Perry)
4th Artillery (Companies A, D, E, G) (Captain Marcus P. Miller)
21st Infantry (Companies B, C, D, E, H, I) (Captain Evan Miles)
Two howitzers, two Gatling guns
Total: 350 soldiers

LOLO TRAIL PURSUIT FORCE, JULY 30, 1877

Brigadier-General Oliver O. Howard
1st Cavalry (Companies B, C, I, K) (Major George Sanford)
4th Artillery (Companies A, C, D, E, G, L, M) (Captain Marcus P. Miller)
21st Infantry (Companies C, D, E, H, I) (Captain Evan Miles)
Company H/8th Infantry
Company C/12th Infantry
Total: 587 soldiers

BATTLE OF THE BIG HOLE, AUGUST 9, 1877

Colonel John Gibbon
7th Infantry (Companies A, D, F, G, I, K)
Civilian volunteers (38)
One 12-pdr howitzer
Total: 154 soldiers and 38 scouts (192)

YELLOWSTONE, SEPTEMBER 9, 1877

Colonel Samuel D. Sturgis
7th Cavalry (Companies F, G, H, I, L, M)
One 12-pdr howitzer
Total: 360

BATTLE OF BEAR PAW, 30 SEPTEMBER 1877

Colonel Nelson A. Miles
2nd Cavalry (Companies F, G, H) (Captain George Tyler)
7th Cavalry (Companies A, D, K) (Captain Owen Hale)
5th Infantry (Companies B, F, G, I, K)
One Hotchkiss gun, one 12-pdr howitzer
Total: 520 soldiers

RIGHT
The Nez Perce warrior Yellow Wolf (Him-mim-mox-mox), with a Winchester repeating rifle. Most of the damage inflicted by the Nez Perce was probably the result of a few dozen experienced and well-armed warriors such as this. (Library of Congress)

NEZ PERCE

Wallowa band (Joseph, Ollokot), 55 warriors
Lamátta band (White Bird), 50 warriors
Alpowai band (Looking Glass), 40 warriors
Pikunan band (Toohoolhoolzote), 30 warriors
Palouse band (Red Elk, Husis Kute), 16 warriors
Total: 190+ warriors

Other war leaders: Yellow Bull (Chuslum Moxmox) and brother Red Elk; Red Owl (Koolkool Snehee), Rainbow (Wahchumyus), and Five Wounds (Pahkatos Owyeen).

OPPOSING PLANS

US ARMY

By the spring of 1877, Brigadier-General Howard's overriding objective was to force the Non-Treaty Nez Perce onto the reservation lands defined by the Treaty of 1863 in order to avoid future outbreaks of violence between the Nez Perce and local American settlers. Until members of the White Bird group began their attacks against settlers along the Salmon River, Howard regarded the Non-Treaty factions as stubborn but not hostile. However once the Non-Treaty Nez Perce murdered American citizens, Howard closed his mind to negotiation and switched to a new set of objectives: the Non-Treaty factions must be defeated and the murderers punished.

General William T. Sherman, commanding general of the US Army in 1877. Sherman was not directly involved in operations during the Nez Perce Campaign but his intent to punish the Nez Perce and any other tribes that demonstrated hostility had a major impact upon the plans made by the field commanders. (Library of Congress)

Initially, Howard believed that his forces could simply pin and crush the Nez Perce, but they proved far too elusive for his small and slow-moving command to nail down. Instead, the operational objective changed to pursuit of the Nez Perce to prevent them from escaping or harming other American citizens. Howard hoped that the fleeing Nez Perce could be cornered in the choke points that they had to pass through, such as the Lolo Pass or Yellowstone National Park. Thus, the US Army soon reverted to the tried doctrine in Indian fighting of converging columns, with Howard trying to coordinate with units stationed in Montana. Tactically, US Army plans hinged on placing a large enough blocking force in the path of the Nez Perce to delay them, while the main pursuit force caught up from behind. This tactic proved simple in theory, but exceedingly difficult in execution. The US Army did benefit from unity of command, even though the campaign was fought across jurisdictional boundaries and the army enjoyed a huge advantage in operational-level command and control thanks to the telegraph.

NEZ PERCE

The Nez Perce suffered throughout the campaign from the lack of unity of command. Authority was based on consensus not on rigid obedience, which turned important decisions into group discussions. Even non-chiefs, such as Poker Joe, were able to exert significant influence over the route and objectives chosen. Furthermore, Joseph was nominally in charge of the Wallowa group – which comprised less than a quarter of the Non-Treaty Nez Perce factions – but his younger brother Ollokot led their warriors on the battlefield.

ABOVE
Nez Perce strategy gradually focused on linking up with the great Sioux war chief Sitting Bull. At the start of the Nez Perce campaign, Looking Glass was apparently unaware that Sitting Bull and his warriors were no longer in Montana but had sought refuge in Canada. However, the Nez Perce believed that Sitting Bull would come to their rescue at Bear Paw and even the US Army was concerned about the Sioux returning to Montana. (Library of Congress)

TOP LEFT
The fate of Custer's men at the Little Bighorn the year before was in the minds of both sides during the Nez Perce Campaign. Early Nez Perce tactical victories only reinforced the notion among other recalcitrant tribes in the Pacific Northwest that there were military options beyond merely submitting to reservation life. (Author's collection)

Nez Perce planning also suffered from an unrealistic appraisal of their situation. Initially, the Non-Treaty factions believed that they were at war with only Howard's troops and the settlers in Idaho – they were shocked to find that US Army troops and settlers in Montana were also hostile. Apparently, many Nez Perce deluded themselves into believing that they could simply lie low in western Montana until Howard gave up the pursuit, then return home. This delusion was fed by the Dreamer philosophy, which foretold that some unknown catastrophe would simply remove the threat posed by the army forever, but belief in miracles makes for poor strategy. Once hostilities began, the only objective for the Non-Treaty factions was to avoid defeat, but the plan simply consisted of putting as much distance between themselves and Howard's troops as possible. Gradually, band leaders decided that they should seek assistance from neighboring tribes but this also proved unrealistic; not only would no other Indians help them, but some tribes such as the Crow and Cheyenne took an active part in helping the US Army pursue them. The utter failure of Nez Perce inter-tribal diplomacy should be seen as a clear precursor to their eventual isolation and military subjugation.

After the battle of the Big Hole and the realization that there was no sanctuary in Montana or among other tribes, the Nez Perce eventually developed the plan of escaping to Canada and joining Sitting Bull's people there. Although renowned for their defeat of Custer, Sitting Bull's Sioux were an eroding force after nearly a year in Canada. Again, this wasn't much of a plan, since it was merely defeat of a different kind – exile rather than subjugation. One of the biggest mistakes that the Nez Perce made was in leaving their native territory in Idaho, where they had the advantage of knowledge of the local terrain and better access to food sources. Once they went on the run, the Nez Perce were forced to move through unfamiliar terrain and starvation became a key factor in their eventual defeat. Given the difficulty the US Army encountered fighting only 30 Shoshone in the rugged mountains east of the Salmon River during the 1879 Sheepeater War, the Nez Perce would have been better advised to make their stand on familiar ground.

OUTBREAK OF THE WAR AND OPENING MOVES (JUNE–JULY 1877)

War is the remedy our enemies have chosen, and I say give them all they want.
General William T. Sherman, 1862

THE MORNING AFTER THE RAIDS

Joseph and a number of other clan chiefs claim to have been absent from the Tolo Lake encampment while their people were going on the warpath – which may have simply been a means of distancing themselves from later accusations of criminal involvement – but when they returned they were faced with dealing with the consequences of mass murder committed by the Nez Perce. Looking Glass was furious and said, "You have acted like fools in murdering white men" and then immediately took his band back to their land on the reservation. Yet the remaining chiefs realized that war was now imminent, so Joseph and White Bird decided to head south 10 miles (16km) to White Bird Canyon, which was more easily defensible. The outbreak of violence had caused further division within the Nez Perce, between those who tried to dissociate themselves from the murders and those who were too guilty to avoid punishment. Apparently it never occurred to Joseph or White Bird

Looking southward down the valley toward the Nez Perce village at White Bird Canyon. Perry's command approached along this route in the pre-dawn darkness. (Author's collection)

Opening moves in Central Idaho, June–July 1877

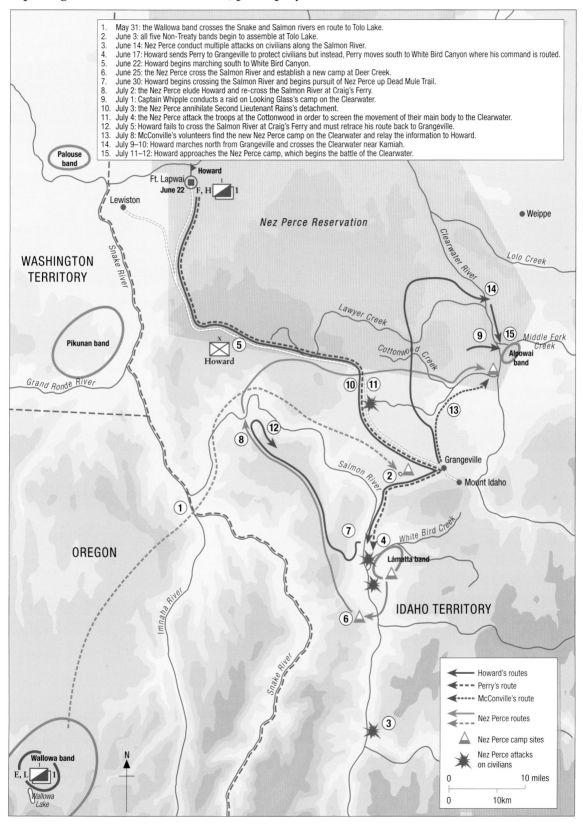

1. May 31: the Wallowa band crosses the Snake and Salmon rivers en route to Tolo Lake.
2. June 3: all five Non-Treaty bands begin to assemble at Tolo Lake.
3. June 14: Nez Perce conduct multiple attacks on civilians along the Salmon River.
4. June 17: Howard sends Perry to Grangeville to protect civilians but instead, Perry moves south to White Bird Canyon where his command is routed.
5. June 22: Howard begins marching south to White Bird Canyon.
6. June 25: the Nez Perce cross the Salmon River and establish a new camp at Deer Creek.
7. June 30: Howard begins crossing the Salmon River and begins pursuit of Nez Perce up Dead Mule Trail.
8. July 2: the Nez Perce elude Howard and re-cross the Salmon River at Craig's Ferry.
9. July 1: Captain Whipple conducts a raid on Looking Glass's camp on the Clearwater.
10. July 3: the Nez Perce annihilate Second Lieutenant Rains's detachment.
11. July 4: the Nez Perce attack the troops at the Cottonwood in order to screen the movement of their main body to the Clearwater.
12. July 5: Howard fails to cross the Salmon River at Craig's Ferry and must retrace his route back to Grangeville.
13. July 8: McConville's volunteers find the new Nez Perce camp on the Clearwater and relay the information to Howard.
14. July 9–10: Howard marches north from Grangeville and crosses the Clearwater near Kamiah.
15. July 11–12: Howard approaches the Nez Perce camp, which begins the battle of the Clearwater.

Colonel Nelson Miles and his staff at the Tongue River Cantonment during the winter of 1876–77. Miles's winter campaign against the Sioux and other plains tribes just months before the outbreak of the Nez Perce War provided him and his troops with invaluable experience in Indian fighting. (Author's collection)

to tell Shore Crossing and Yellow Bull to vanish into the mountains while the rest of the Non-Treaty factions moved immediately onto the reservation, which might have avoided open warfare. Instead, they elected to protect the murderers and everything that followed was a result of the deliberate Nez Perce effort to shield a handful of their tribe from criminal prosecution.

At Fort Lapwai, Howard first received word of the attacks on the afternoon of June 15 and immediately dispatched two cavalry companies under Captain David L. Perry to protect the 100 civilians around Grangeville and Mount Idaho. Howard was not certain of the extent of the outbreak and limited his initial call for reinforcements to recalling two other companies of the 1st Cavalry from the Wallowa Valley and three companies of the 21st Infantry from Fort Walla Walla. He was reluctant to call for outside help – which could reflect badly on his handling of the situation – until Perry provided more information about Nez Perce intentions. After a trek of 50 miles (80km) down the Lewiston–Mount Idaho Road, Perry arrived at Grangeville around 2000hrs on June 16. Although his orders were only to protect the town, the civilians were angry about the Nez Perce attacks and demanded that Perry take some punitive measures against them. At this point, Perry demonstrated a serious deficiency in leadership and allowed the civilians in Grangeville to dictate his course of action to him. Without resting his troops, Perry headed south 17 miles (27km) toward White Bird Canyon, along with a small group of armed civilian volunteers.

BATTLE OF WHITE BIRD CANYON

Perry arrived at the entrance to White Bird Canyon around 0400hrs on the morning of June 17. His command consisted of 103 cavalrymen, three friendly Nez Perce scouts and 11 armed civilian volunteers. Based upon general knowledge from the civilians that the Nez Perce were encamped along White Bird Creek, Perry conducted a movement to contact without any fixed plan regarding what he intended to do once he found the hostiles. He had no orders from Howard to engage the Nez Perce or to negotiate with them. Nevertheless, he headed southward with his own Company F in the lead, followed by Captain Joel Trimble's Company H, toward two prominent rises with a saddle depression in between. An advance detachment, led by First Lieutenant Edward Theller, scouted about 200 yards (180m) ahead of the main body. By this point, the troops had been in the saddle for hours, having gone two nights without sleep and the rugged terrain they were moving over was tiring to both man and horse, which meant that Perry's weary command went into action in an exhausted condition. On the approach march, one of the soldiers foolishly lit his pipe, which was spotted by a Nez Perce scout. Perry had no real plan of action and Sergeant Michael McCarthy later said, "If there was any plan of attack, I never heard of it."

Thanks to the faulty light discipline of the 1st Cavalry troopers, the Nez Perce were now aware that soldiers were coming and they deployed two groups of warriors to protect the most likely avenues of approach. Ollokot led the larger group of about 50 warriors, some mounted and some dismounted, guarding the west side of the valley. A smaller group of 15 warriors under Two Moon screened the eastern side of the village. Nez Perce sources admit

TOP
The twin hills overlooking the Nez Perce village. Perry's command inclined toward the left hill, while Ollokot's mounted warriors were deployed toward the right. (Author's collection)

BOTTOM
The view atop the left hill where Perry's Company F formed a skirmish line. The Nez Perce village was down in the trees below, along the river. (Author's collection)

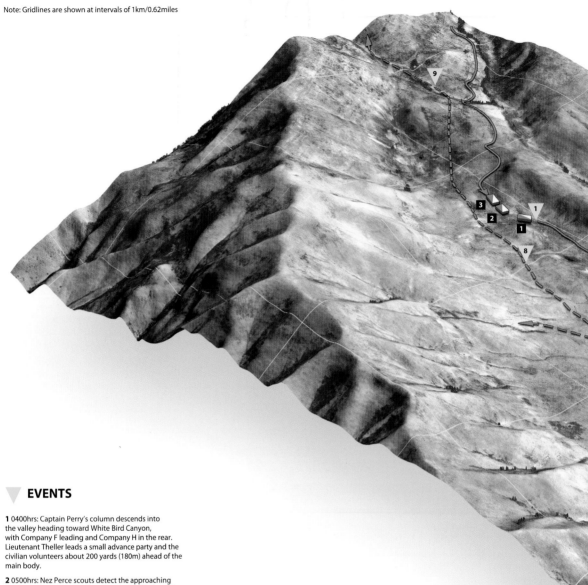

▼ EVENTS

1 0400hrs: Captain Perry's column descends into the valley heading toward White Bird Canyon, with Company F leading and Company H in the rear. Lieutenant Theller leads a small advance party and the civilian volunteers about 200 yards (180m) ahead of the main body.

2 0500hrs: Nez Perce scouts detect the approaching cavalry and two groups of warriors are hastily formed to defend the village. Ollokot takes 50 warriors to defend the western approach to the village while Two Moon has a smaller group of 15 to defend the eastern approaches.

3 0615hrs: as they approach the crest, Theller spots the Indian pony herd, but not the village. Shortly afterwards, the civilian volunteers open fire on five mounted Nez Perce approaching to parley.

4 0630hrs: Perry deploys his command on line along the crest of the ridge, with Company F forming a dismounted skirmish line in the center.

5 The civilian volunteers rush toward White Bird Creek but run straight into an ambush by Two Moon's warriors. After suffering a few casualties, the volunteers retreat in disorder and Two Moon's group occupies their vacated knoll and pours enfilade fire into Perry's left flank. Meanwhile, Ollokot begins an encircling movement against Perry's right flank and warriors in the village begin joining the action.

6 0700hrs: both companies begin to fall back without orders and Perry's left collapses in a panic. In desperation, Sergeant McCarthy is sent with six troops to hold a piece of rocky high ground on Perry's right to delay Ollokot's pursuit.

7 Perry tries to re-form a line at the next piece of high ground to the north, but Ollokot's warriors quickly disperse the troopers. Perry's command scatters in headlong retreat.

8 Ollokot mounts a vigorous pursuit and chases the fragments of Perry's command for more than 5 miles (8km). Wounded cavalrymen are abandoned and killed by the Nez Perce.

9 About 0800hrs: during the retreat, Lieutenant Theller leads a group of seven troops into a steep ravine, where they are trapped and killed in a desperate last stand.

BATTLE OF WHITE BIRD CANYON, JUNE 17, 1877
The Nez Perce rout the 1st Cavalry.

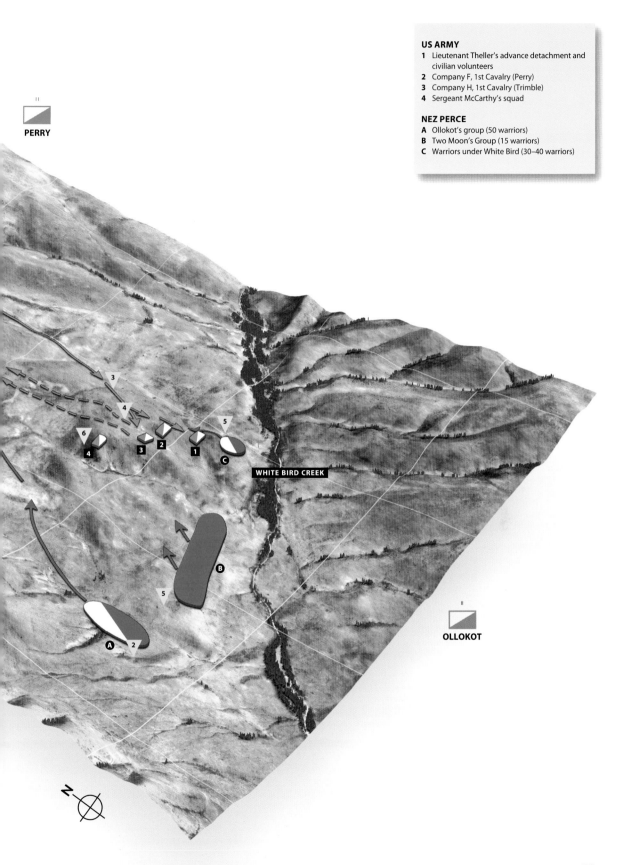

PERRY

WHITE BIRD CREEK

OLLOKOT

35

TOP
The view of the cavalry's position from the Nez Perce position. The civilian volunteers were driven off the cone-shaped hill early in the battle, which allowed the Nez Perce to enfilade Perry's skirmish line. (Author's collection)

BOTTOM
The view from McCarthy's Point looking toward the Nez Perce village. Sergeant McCarthy was posted here with six soldiers, but was unable to stop Ollokot's envelopment from the right. (Author's collection)

that a large number of warriors were still drunk or hung-over after the week of carousing and were unable to take part in the coming battle, so the total number of warriors available was fewer than 100. Joseph, who played only a small role in the battle, dispatched a six-man mounted patrol toward the approaching soldiers – either to parley or to get more information on the threat. The Nez Perce were confident, well rested and operating on familiar terrain, which gave them a number of advantages over Perry's men.

At about 0615hrs, Lt. Theller and his scouts approached the crest of the easternmost ridge and spotted part of the Nez Perce pony herd but not the village, which was hidden by intervening terrain. The mounted Nez Perce group spotted Theller's scouts and rode toward them but one of the attached civilian volunteers, Arthur Chapman, fired on them. Modern Nez Perce cite this incident to claim that Americans fired the first shot in the war, conveniently ignoring their own murder of 18 American citizens within the previous four days. Furthermore, Perry's troops had no reason to believe that the Nez Perce were anything but hostile after the death of these civilians, so firing on the supposed parley group was not as unjustified as has been claimed. Rather than blaming Perry for starting a war that *ipso facto* had already begun, he should be judged harshly for rushing into battle with tired troops and no tactical plan.

Sergeant Michael McCarthy, the senior NCO in Company H, 1st Cavalry, at the battle of White Bird Canyon. The 32-year-old Newfoundland-born sergeant was left to conduct a hopeless rearguard as Perry's command disintegrated and he was the only survivor of his squad. Cut off and abandoned, McCarthy succeeded in rejoining his unit at Grangeville two days later, for which he was awarded the Medal of Honor in 1897. (Author's collection)

Hearing the shots fired, Perry immediately rushed the main body forward and began deploying Company F in a dismounted skirmish line along the crest of the ridge. Captain Trimble's Company H began to occupy the right of Perry's line but was still mounted when the action began in earnest. There was also a gap of almost 200 yards (180m) between the two companies, which made it difficult for Perry to control his force. Below them, the Nez Perce village was still hidden behind a series of conical-shaped hills, so Perry's troops could only engage the small groups of Nez Perce warriors who were rushing toward the sound of firing. Perry proved a poor tactician, engaging a foe with the rising sun in his eyes while his own men were silhouetted against the crest of the ridge. He also deployed his skirmish line in open terrain, while ignoring a rock outcropping just 30 yards (27m) to his rear that would have provided excellent cover.

Meanwhile, several of the civilian volunteers rashly chased after the retreating parley group but ran straight into an ambush by Two Moon's warriors. After taking a few casualties, the volunteers retreated in disorder and Two Moon's group moved forward to occupy a raised knoll on Perry's left flank. From this knoll, the Nez Perce sharpshooters poured a deadly enfilade fire into the flank of Company F, killing seven soldiers in the opening moments of the action. Perry's men could barely see Two Moon's warriors, who were firing from dead space and concealed by waist-high grass. With both companies on line, Perry's troops fired several ragged volleys toward their front, while virtually ignoring the threat on their flank. When Perry's trumpeter was killed by a lucky hit, he lost any remaining ability to influence the troops who were more than a few yards from him. Shore Crossing and his friend Red Moccasin Tops, the two responsible for the initial murders that started the war, were part of Two Moon's group and they wore full-length red blanket coats intended to show their contempt for the soldiers.

While Two Moon was disrupting Perry's left flank, Ollokot's mounted warriors began a wide enveloping sweep around the right flank, out of range of Company H's carbines. Some warriors were also joining from the village, which kept Perry's attention focused to his front. After less than 30 minutes of combat, Perry's command began to disintegrate as more troops were hit by the accurate Nez Perce fire and the realization dawned that they were about to be encircled. The panic began with a few troops on the left falling back without orders but, as the skirmish line dwindled, it was soon every man for himself. The flat area behind the ridgeline was devoid of any cover and the fleeing troops were easy prey for the on-rushing mounted warriors. In desperation, Capt. Trimble sent Sgt. Michael McCarthy and six troopers to hold a piece of rocky high ground on Perry's right to delay Ollokot's

LIEUTENANT THELLER'S LAST STAND, JUNE 17, 1877 (pp. 38–39)

The movement to contact by two troops of the 1st US Cavalry under Captain Perry to the Nez Perce camp at White Bird Canyon quickly resulted in an unexpectedly fierce engagement, followed by a precipitous rout. The troopers of Companies F and H fell back in small groups, pursued by mounted Nez Perce warriors. Quite quickly, the cavalry troops lost all cohesion and it was virtually every man for himself. First Lieutenant Edward R. Theller (1831–77), on loan from the 21st Infantry, had been given command of a squad-sized formation that acted as an advanced guard for Perry's command as it advanced to White Bird Canyon, but which now found itself abandoned in the headlong retreat. Fleeing up the valley in the wake of their routed comrades, Theller led a group of seven cavalrymen into a dead-end ravine and before they could escape, they were surrounded by a larger group of Nez Perce warriors **(1)**.

Lieutenant Theller's men formed a small perimeter at the bottom of the ravine and hoped for rescue, but Capt. Perry was unaware that Theller's group had become isolated. Theller's men fought back hard, keeping the Nez Perce at bay for a while, until their carbine ammunition was expended. Constant Nez Perce fire from above wounded several of the soldiers and most of their horses **(2)**, effectively ending all hope of escape. Once the soldiers reverted to their shorter-range Colt pistols, the Nez Perce warriors gradually closed in and Lt .Theller was killed by a bullet to his brain from an enemy marksman **(3)**. The last soldiers continued firing until all were hit by Nez Perce fire. The Nez Perce then closed in and finished off the wounded. Despite the image of victims that Nez Perce spokesmen have promoted since their defeat, Nez Perce warriors were quite vicious on the battlefield and rarely took prisoners. Most of the dead were also mutilated.

pursuit while the rest of the command skedaddled back 200 yards (180m) to the next hill mass. McCarthy's detachment sniped at Ollokot's warriors and managed to wound one or two of them, which succeeded in delaying the Nez Perce pursuit for a few vital moments. However, once McCarthy and his men tried to retreat across the open ground to rejoin their fleeing comrades, Ollokot's mounted warriors killed every soldier but McCarthy, who succeeded in evading them.

Perry tried to re-form a line at the next piece of high ground to the north, but Ollokot's warriors pressed them hard and quickly dispersed the troopers. After that, Perry's command scattered in headlong retreat and all cohesion was lost. Ollokot's pursuit was vigorous, brutal and effective, hounding the fragments of Perry's command for more than 5 miles (8km). Wounded cavalrymen who could not flee were killed by Ollokot's warriors and some of the bodies were mutilated. Sergeant Patrick Gunn of Company F was later found with his severed genitals stuffed in his mouth, the apparent victim of torture. In one of the final actions, Lt. Theller and seven soldiers retreated into a steep ravine where they were soon pinned down by Nez Perce fire from above. After a desperate last stand, all eight cavalrymen were killed. No prisoners were taken. Perry's survivors huddled in Grangeville for a week, adding scant comfort to the worried civilians.

The battle of White Bird Canyon was a tactical triumph for the Nez Perce. In less than an hour, they had routed two cavalry companies and killed 34 soldiers, while suffering only three lightly wounded themselves. However, any possibility for negotiating with Howard was now gone and the Nez Perce leaders realized that they would soon face a full-scale military campaign against themselves, a war which they could hardly expect to win. Back at Fort Lapwai, the defeated Perry blamed the defeat on the collapse of the civilian volunteers but this was merely an excuse, since his right flank was unable to prevent Ollokot's encirclement. Indeed, it is probably fortuitous that Perry's command routed when it did because otherwise it would have been pinned and annihilated by Ollokot's maneuver. Furthermore, Perry exaggerated the numbers of Nez Perce warriors engaged and omitted the fact that his own troops had enjoyed a five-to-one numerical advantage in the opening moments of the battle.

HOWARD'S FUMBLED PURSUIT

When two of Perry's routed troops arrived back at Fort Lapwai, Howard was shocked both by the amount of casualties and the ferocity of Nez Perce resistance. Clearly he was not dealing with a few hotheads, but an armed and unpredictable opponent. As department commander, Howard immediately ordered more companies of the 1st Cavalry, the 21st Infantry and the 4th Artillery to assemble at Fort Lapwai, although it would take weeks for most to arrive. By June 22, he had amassed a mixed force of 227 troops and he decided to take to the field before most of his reinforcements arrived in order to forestall being replaced by a more experienced Indian fighter, such as Brigadier-General George Crook. He deliberately ordered Colonel Alfred Sully, the highly experienced commander of the 21st Infantry, to stay behind and guard Lewiston while taking six of his companies. Howard headed southward from Fort Lapwai with his small command, but with only a small pack train and his logistic preparations soon proved inadequate.

The ravine where First Lieutenant Edward R. Theller and his ten soldiers were wiped out during the retreat from White Bird Canyon. (Author's collection)

After rendezvousing with Perry at Grangeville on June 25, Howard's force approached the entrance to White Bird Canyon in pouring rain on the afternoon of June 27. The bodies of Perry's dead troops were found and buried, but in the ten days since the battle the Nez Perce had slipped unhindered to the west side of the Salmon River and established a new camp at Deer Creek. Howard was now on the wrong side of the river and he fumbled about for the next two days, uncertain what to do. Four dismounted companies of the 4th Artillery and another infantry company joined his command while he bivouacked on the White Bird Canyon battlefield, but Howard still had barely 400 troops and he was uncertain about Nez Perce intentions. Ollokot sent some of his warriors to the west side of the Salmon River to skirmish with Howard's pickets and to taunt them to try and cross. However, the soldiers only succeeded in fatally shooting one of their own pickets by accident in the dark. Many of Howard's soldiers were spooked sleeping on the site of Perry's defeat and expected a Nez Perce attack at any moment, so no fires were lit at night. Furthermore, Howard had rushed from Fort Lapwai so quickly that the troops were forced to sleep out in the mud and rain without tents or blankets. Any army sitting on their hands in drenching rain within sight of a confident enemy and subsisting on cold food is likely to suffer from low morale, which quickly undermined the effectiveness of Howard's troops. Meanwhile, the Nez Perce warriors could return to their warm lodges for ample food and rest.

On June 30, after nearly three days of inactivity, Howard finally gathered up the gumption to move to the bank of the Salmon River but rather than attempting a crossing at the narrowest and easiest point near the junction with White Bird Creek, he made the ridiculous decision to move north 1½ miles (2km) and cross at some rapids. Throughout the campaign, Howard consistently acted like topography did not exist and his maneuver required the troops to cross a steep, 3,300ft-high (1,000m) ridgeline with wagons, mules and artillery. What should have taken less than a day – crossing a 330ft-

Caught in a circle by Charles Schreyvogel. The last stands of lieutenants Theller and Rains were similar, with small groups of isolated cavalrymen holding off circling Indians until their ammunition ran out. By the time that the warriors closed in to finish them off, most of the soldiers were wounded. (Library of Congress)

wide (100m) river – took three days because Howard would not attempt it until he had artillery support on hand, so the crossing was not completed until July 2. With the troops thoroughly exhausted, Howard then advanced south toward Deer Creek but found the Nez Perce were long gone. The three-day river crossing had given the Nez Perce ample time to pack up their camp and head to the northwest, away from Howard. In just 36 hours, the Nez Perce marched 25 miles (40km) across the mountains and re-crossed the Salmon River at Craig's Ferry. The Nez Perce conducted this retreat with women and children, along with about 3,000 head of horse. Foolishly, Howard had not even sent scouts across the river to maintain contact with the enemy, so once he crossed he realized that he had no idea where they were.

Howard had lost contact with the enemy and he thought they might have split up, with some heading south to the Wallowa Valley and others westward to the Snake River. Following the unmistakable trail left by thousands of Nez Perce horses, Howard drove his troops up "Dead Mule Trail," whose steep 45-degree slopes earned their sobriquet by causing the death of many of his pack mules. Lieutenant Charles Wood described conditions on the trail as simply: "Rain. Mud. Bombarded with [falling] pack mules. Sleeping in water." It took Howard's column four days to reach Craig's Ferry on the Salmon River but when they tried a crossing on July 5, raging waters swept away the few available rafts and even the cavalry could not cross. Howard spent a day impotently fumbling at the river's edge, with the troops wondering how Nez Perce women and children could accomplish what they could not, then turned around and began a grueling and morale-crushing retreat to the crossing site at White Bird Creek. Howard marched ahead with the cavalry to reach Grangeville, but the infantry and artillery did not get across the Salmon River until July 8–9. During the retrograde march, supply arrangements fell apart and the troops were reduced to eating berries or just went hungry. Howard had not only been outmaneuvered and allowed the Nez Perce to get well ahead of him, but he had also wasted more than a week in futile marching and exhausted his troops to no end.

WIDENING THE WAR

Angry about the delay in crossing the Salmon River and apprehensive about more Nez Perce joining Joseph and White Bird, Howard made an incredibly foolish decision to launch a pre-emptive strike on the camp of Chief Looking Glass on the Clearwater River. Despite the fact that Looking Glass had refused to join the other Non-Treaty factions and his people were on reservation land as Howard had directed, Howard became convinced owing to rumors from local settlers that they were a threat. On June 30 Howard ordered Captain Stephen G. Whipple, with 66 troops from Companies E and L, 1st Cavalry, to raid Looking Glass's camp and arrest him. Whipple attacked a nearly defenseless village on the morning of July 1 and killed three Nez Perce, but failed to arrest Looking Glass. Instead, Looking Glass now decided to join the other Non-Treaty factions on the warpath, further widening the war. Howard's attack on Looking Glass was utter stupidity.

Once Howard was across the Salmon River and realized that the Nez Perce had eluded him, he became very concerned about his lines of communication. He sent a courier to Capt. Whipple ordering him to take his two cavalry companies, along with two Gatling guns, to establish a defensive position at Norton's Ranch near Cottonwood to protect the supply convoys passing by from Lewiston. He also ordered Whipple to send scouts to look for the Nez Perce in case they got across the Salmon River. While Howard's column was stumbling along Dead Mule Trail 15 miles (24km) to the south, the Nez Perce advanced from Craig's Ferry toward the northeast, heading to their home ground on the Clearwater. Along the way, they had to cross the Lewiston–Mount Idaho road and passed close by the Cottonwood. On the morning of July 3, Whipple's scouts detected the approaching Nez Perce. Whipple ordered rifle pits dug around Norton's Ranch and positioned the two Gatling guns on a prominent rise, then gathered most of his cavalry for a sortie against the Nez Perce. He sent Second Lieutenant Sevier M. Rains ahead with an advance guard of ten cavalrymen and two scouts, then followed at a distance with 70 more troopers. Around 1900hrs, Rains's squad passed by a large group of mounted Nez Perce led by Five Wounds and Rainbow, who were concealed in some low ground. Suddenly, the Nez Perce were between Rains's squad and Whipple's main body and before Rains could react, a large enemy force attacked his small group from behind. One veteran Nez Perce warrior named Wat-zam-yas, apparently armed with a repeating rifle, killed four of the soldiers in the opening moments of the action. Although Rains's men dismounted and put up a stiff fight behind some rocks, all were killed within a matter of minutes. Whipple's main body stopped within 880 yards (800m) of Rains – whom they could not see because of intervening terrain – and listened while the advance guard was massacred. No Nez Perce casualties were suffered in the brief action. Once again, the Nez Perce took no prisoners and later some admitted that the wounded were beaten to death. Sensing a large enemy force nearby, Whipple refused to move to support Rains and then retreated to Norton's Ranch.

On the morning of July 4, Capt. Perry led a large pack mule train from Fort Lapwai into Norton's Ranch and took charge of the garrison, which now numbered 120 troops. At this point, the main Nez Perce body of noncombatants and horses began to move past this army post in the distance and the Nez Perce warriors decided to conduct an action to prevent the cavalry from interfering with this movement. Around 1330hrs, about

100 Nez Perce warriors appeared within sight of Norton's Ranch and opened a steady harassing fire. The Nez Perce then did a very unusual thing in Indian warfare – they attacked a fortified position held by regular troops. Cavalrymen fired back from shallow rifle pits with their carbines and the Gatling guns fired several volleys at mounted warriors, but both weapons were too short-ranged to be effective. The Nez Perce proved adept at using dead space to get close to the post but retreated whenever they came under heavy fire. After seven hours of sustained sniping, the Nez Perce finally broke off the action around 2100hrs. Amazingly, neither side had suffered any casualties, but the Nez Perce had succeeded in neutralizing Whipple's force while their noncombatants crossed the Lewiston–Mount Idaho Road. Small groups of Nez Perce continued to harass the cavalry at Norton's Ranch the next morning until their people had gotten further away. By chance, a 17-man force of civilian volunteers approached from Mount Idaho and 20 mounted Nez Perce intercepted them a mile short of the ranch. One Nez Perce warrior was killed – their first combat fatality of the war – but the volunteers lost several of their horses and were pinned down in a creek. It was clear that the volunteers would be annihilated once their ammunition ran out, but Perry hesitated to act. He was probably still rattled from the defeat at White Bird Canyon and his leadership at Cottonwood was ineffectual. When some of his sergeants threatened to go help the volunteers on their own, Perry finally relented and allowed Capt. Whipple to sortie with 60 cavalrymen. Having killed or wounded five of the volunteers, the Nez Perce withdrew as Whipple approached and allowed him to bring the mauled volunteers into Norton's Ranch.

Although Perry and Whipple had prevented Howard's vital pack train from falling into Nez Perce hands, they had absolutely failed to stop the hostiles from moving their entire main body past them to the Camas Prairie. Two days after the fight with the volunteers, the Nez Perce reached the Clearwater River, where they linked up with Looking Glass's group, bringing the total number of hostiles to 740, including at least 200 warriors. The various bands of the Non-Treaty Nez Perce were now united, at their strongest and on familiar terrain. Believing that Howard had given up the pursuit, the Nez Perce set up a village on the riverbank and reverted to a fairly non-warlike posture, but did build some log breastworks facing to the southwest. Having eluded Howard and Perry, they seemed to regard the war as good as over.

BATTLE OF THE CLEARWATER

While Howard was fumbling about trying to get back across the Salmon River and Perry was sitting on his hands at Norton's Ranch, it was the armed civilian volunteers under Colonel Edward McConville who took up the pursuit of the Nez Perce. The 31-year-old McConville was no amateur; he had fought as a Union cavalryman during the Civil War and then fought Apaches in Arizona before retiring to Idaho in 1873. Volunteers had been coming in from Lewiston, Mount Idaho, Grangeville and other towns since word of the initial Nez Perce raids went out and by July 8 McConville had gathered 75 men at Norton's Ranch. On his own initiative, he sent scouts out to follow the Nez Perce trail past the post and they soon discovered the new village on the Clearwater. McConville's volunteers occupied a hill on the west side of the

Battle of the Clearwater, July 11, 1877

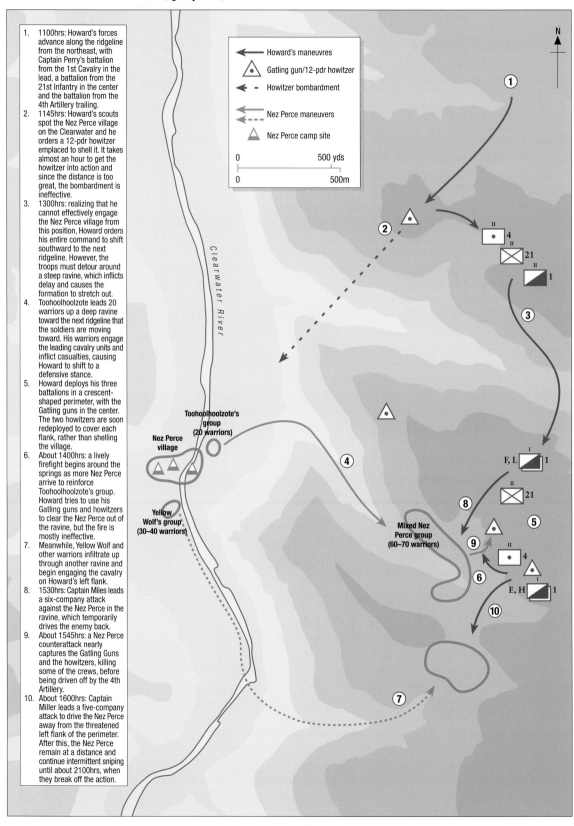

1. 1100hrs: Howard's forces advance along the ridgeline from the northeast, with Captain Perry's battalion from the 1st Cavalry in the lead, a battalion from the 21st Infantry in the center and the battalion from the 4th Artillery trailing.

2. 1145hrs: Howard's scouts spot the Nez Perce village on the Clearwater and he orders a 12-pdr howitzer emplaced to shell it. It takes almost an hour to get the howitzer into action and since the distance is too great, the bombardment is ineffective.

3. 1300hrs: realizing that he cannot effectively engage the Nez Perce village from this position, Howard orders his entire command to shift southward to the next ridgeline. However, the troops must detour around a steep ravine, which inflicts delay and causes the formation to stretch out.

4. Toohoolhoolzote leads 20 warriors up a deep ravine toward the next ridgeline that the soldiers are moving toward. His warriors engage the leading cavalry units and inflict casualties, causing Howard to shift to a defensive stance.

5. Howard deploys his three battalions in a crescent-shaped perimeter, with the Gatling guns in the center. The two howitzers are soon redeployed to cover each flank, rather than shelling the village.

6. About 1400hrs: a lively firefight begins around the springs as more Nez Perce arrive to reinforce Toohoolhoolzote's group. Howard tries to use his Gatling guns and howitzers to clear the Nez Perce out of the ravine, but the fire is mostly ineffective.

7. Meanwhile, Yellow Wolf and other warriors infiltrate up through another ravine and begin engaging the cavalry on Howard's left flank.

8. 1530hrs: Captain Miles leads a six-company attack against the Nez Perce in the ravine, which temporarily drives the enemy back.

9. About 1545hrs: a Nez Perce counterattack nearly captures the Gatling Guns and the howitzers, killing some of the crews, before being driven off by the 4th Artillery.

10. About 1600hrs: Captain Miller leads a five-company attack to drive the Nez Perce away from the threatened left flank of the perimeter. After this, the Nez Perce remain at a distance and continue intermittent sniping until about 2100hrs, when they break off the action.

Howard's maneuvres

Gatling gun/12-pdr howitzer

Howitzer bombardment

Nez Perce maneuvers

Nez Perce camp site

0   500 yds
0   500m

Clearwater River

Toohoolhoolzote's group (20 warriors)

Nez Perce village

Yellow Wolf's group (30–40 warriors)

Mixed Nez Perce group (60–70 warriors)

F, L   1

21

E, H   1

4

Clearwater from which they could monitor the Nez Perce village and sent couriers to provide Howard with the location of the hostile camp. McConville's volunteers then sat back and waited for the army to arrive.

Howard was at Grangeville when McConville's courier found him on July 9 and he ordered his tired troops to advance northward to the Clearwater. However, in the meantime, the undisciplined volunteers accidentally gave away their location and the alerted Nez Perce warriors swarmed around their position, which soon became known as "Misery Hill." The Nez Perce succeeded in capturing about half the volunteers' horses but were unwilling to risk casualties in a pitched battle and were content merely to keep McConville's men pinned down with sniper fire for two days. Eventually, the volunteers ran out of food and water but the Nez Perce had grown careless. McConville led his men off the hill and withdrew when the Nez Perce were inattentive, but this meant that the volunteers were not in a position to cooperate with Howard's approaching column.

Even though the courier from McConville provided Howard with the exact position of the Nez Perce village, his approach to the Clearwater was more of a blind probe than a direct stab at the enemy. Howard's column reached the village of Kamiah on July 10 and crossed the south fork of the Clearwater at Jackson's Bridge, north of the Nez Perce village and on the wrong side of the river. On the morning of July 11, Howard's column ascended a long, wooded ridgeline on the east side of the river and began advancing in the general direction of Looking Glass's old camp, which was actually heading away from the Nez Perce village. Captain Perry's battalion from the 1st Cavalry was in the lead, with Captain Evan Miles's battalion from the 21st Infantry in the center, followed by Captain Marcus P. Miller's battalion from the 4th Artillery.

Almost by accident, one of Howard's aides looked over his shoulder and saw the Nez Perce village in the distance, on the opposite bank of the river. Despite his muddled approach march, Howard had actually gained the advantage of surprise because the Nez Perce scouts were looking southward toward where McConville's volunteers had been, rather than toward the northeast. However, Howard decided to order one of his 12-pdr howitzers emplaced on a ridgeline overlooking the village. By 1245hrs the howitzer was able to fire a couple of shells at the village, but the range was too great so the bombardment served only to alert the Nez Perce. A single Nez Perce warrior, Mean Man (Howwallits), was wounded by one of the howitzer shells.

Frustrated, Howard ordered his entire command to shift southward to the next ridgeline so that his artillery could strike the village. However, his troops had to detour around a steep ravine, which required another hour to accomplish and which caused his formation to elongate. In doing this, Howard violated some of the most basic concepts of tactical maneuvering in the presence of the enemy. First, he committed his main body to action without adequate reconnaissance, then he squandered the advantage of surprise, finally he conducted a lateral movement across an alerted enemy's front, which invited a devastating flank attack against his strung-out forces in rough terrain.

Although caught somewhat by surprise, the Nez Perce reacted to the threat with great alacrity and intrepidity. It was the aged Toohoolhoolzote who gathered up 20 warriors and led them up a deep, wooded ravine toward the ridgeline that the soldiers were approaching. It was a race for key terrain not unlike the race for Cemetery Hill in 1863, but this time Howard lost the race. Toohoolhoolzote's warriors were able to fire upon the leading cavalry units, which disrupted the formation of a coherent line. Second Lieutenant Harry L. Bailey noted that Indian infiltrators soon surrounded his Company B, 21st Infantry, forcing the soldiers to establish an all-around defense. Bailey also noted that even though the Nez Perce managed to get within 100 yards (90m) of his position that "we could seldom see any Indians" owing to their clever use of cover and concealment. However the soldiers were almost totally exposed on top of the rocky and barren bluffs, being forced to lie down to reduce casualties from the steady sniper fire. Some warriors even managed to rush forward and capture part of the pack train, loaded with howitzer ammunition. More warriors under Ollokot and Rainbow followed up the steep ravines, sometimes engaging the soldiers at point-blank range before falling back. With his vanguard already assuming a defensive posture, Howard tried to establish a crescent-shaped formation with his howitzers on the flanks and the Gatling guns in his center. His intent was to form a powerful skirmish line, augmented by artillery, which would decimate the Nez Perce attackers. Owing to poor command and control, the 4th Artillery and 21st Infantry accidentally fired upon each other, inflicting several casualties.

However, the Nez Perce did not play by Howard's rules. Instead of tackling the soldiers head-on, they infiltrated along their flanks, using the wooded ravine for cover. By 1400hrs the Nez Perce had over 100 warriors in the fight, operating in small, dispersed groups. Howard ordered his Gatling guns to fire into the ravines to clear out the infiltrators, but their barrage was ineffective. With the artillery under a continued galling sniper fire, around 1530hrs Captain Evan Miles led most of his infantrymen in a charge against the Nez Perce in the ravine, temporarily driving them back. Yet no sooner had the soldiers returned to their position than the Nez Perce infiltrators

Dead Mule Trail, as depicted on the cover of Harper's Weekly on September 29, 1877. Howard's troops spent the better part of a week crossing then recrossing this exhausting terrain, all to no end. Howard's logistic arrangements were poor to begin with and once much of his mule train was lost on this trail, his troops were reduced to foraging. (Library of Congress)

returned and mounted a bold attack against Howard's exposed artillery. Nez Perce sharpshooters managed to kill or wound all but one gunner at one 12-pdr and nearly captured a Gatling gun. In desperation, Captain Marcus Miller launched a five-company attack with his artillerymen that drove the Nez Perce away from the threatened left flank of the perimeter. Nevertheless, the constant Nez Perce attacks on the artillery batteries forced Howard to pull them further back, which meant they could no longer shell the village. After this, the Nez Perce remained at a distance and continued intermittent sniping until about 2100hrs, when they broke off the action.

The willingness of the Nez Perce to engage in a protracted, nine-hour close-quarter battle with the US Army was highly unusual in Indian warfare, but the resolution of the Nez Perce deserted them during the night. Although Yellow Bull and a few others built stonewalled fighting positions in the ravine to block the soldiers' access to their village, many other warriors returned to their lodges. Here, the lack of discipline weighed in against the Nez Perce, since warriors could come and go from the battlefield as they pleased. Meanwhile, the soldiers were digging shallow trenches atop the bluffs during the night, but went without food and suffered from lack of water. Howard made a serious mistake in not conducting any reconnaissance during the night or sending his cavalry to cross the river to go after the Nez Perce pony herd.

As the sun rose, sniping resumed around 0600hrs and the soldiers made a determined effort to seize a fresh water spring located in the ravine. After three hours of creeping forward, the artillerymen captured the spring and the parched soldiers could refill their canteens and brew coffee. Howard was resolved to conduct a deliberate assault on the village with his infantry and artillery, but issued no orders for the next nine hours. Instead, a minor skirmish erupted on the right flank around 1500hrs when Miller's artillerymen moved to support a supply train approaching from Fort Lapwai

Infantry deployed in skirmish line, with the company first sergeant breaking open another box of ammunition. Unlike this idealized Frederic Remington print, troops at the Clearwater were forced to fire mostly from prone or kneeling positions in order to survive under Indian sniper fire. Furthermore, smoke from so many black powder weapons being fired in close proximity made command and control difficult, resulting in at least one incident of fratricide with one company firing upon its neighbor. (Author's collection)

THE FIGHT FOR THE HOWITZER AT THE CLEARWATER, JULY 11, 1877 (pp. 50–51)

When Howard found the Nez Perce village on the banks of the Clearwater River on July 11, he tried to use his superior firepower to overawe the enemy, rather than to close with them. In addition to two Gatling guns **(1)**, Howard had two 12-pdr mountain howitzers **(2)**, which he used to bombard the village from extreme range. However this bombardment failed to inflict any significant casualties upon the Nez Perce and provoked a violent counterattack by two groups of dismounted Nez Perce warriors, who rapidly moved up two ravines toward Howard's troops atop the ridgeline.

Howard deployed his two howitzers and Gatling gun on line, supported by several companies of infantry, but they were unable to stop the Nez Perce infiltration up the wooded ravines

and the crews from Battery E, 4th Artillery, soon came under accurate small-arms fire. The Nez Perce began to attack in small groups of four to five warriors each **(3)**, which presented fleeting and poor targets for either the howitzers or Gatling guns. Finally, a determined Nez Perce got close enough to shoot five of the six crew members of one howitzer, but Private William S. LeMay **(4)** crouched behind the wheels and fired the piece, temporarily driving off the Nez Perce. Another group of Nez Perce nearly overran the Gatling guns. With their artillery in danger, the artillerymen of Battery E under First Lieutenant Charles F. Humphrey led a desperate charge with a dozen men and managed to drive the Nez Perce warriors back just before the guns were overrun.

and discovered that the Indian reaction was surprisingly feeble. Pushing several companies into the ravine, Miller suddenly found that he was facing only a tiny rearguard of Nez Perce warriors and he ordered a pursuit to the river's edge. It soon became apparent that the Nez Perce had used the respite to evacuate all of the noncombatants away from Howard's force, leaving only a small rearguard to deceive and delay. Howard pushed his infantry forward to the banks of the Clearwater but it was too deep for them to cross and by the time that Perry's cavalrymen crossed, the Nez Perce were long gone.

Howard had not only failed to inflict any serious damage on the Nez Perce, but he had once again also allowed them to escape after a battle in which the army had clearly gotten the worst of it. In total, Howard's force suffered 15 dead and 25 wounded – a casualty rate of nearly ten percent – but had inflicted only four killed and six wounded on the Nez Perce. The primary target, the Nez Perce pony herd, was never seriously threatened. Fearful of the political consequences of another failure, Howard sent a deliberately deceptive report of the battle, which claimed about 70 Nez Perce casualties, direct to Washington. Howard's lies allowed him to stay in command, but it did not change the fact that he had not accomplished any part of his mission. For their part, the Nez Perce had passed up their one possible chance to end the war on their own terms. If the Nez Perce had committed all 200 warriors on the first day, Howard's strung-out forces might have been defeated in detail and the survivors besieged atop the hill. A clear-cut Nez Perce victory would have resulted in Howard's relief and bought time for some kind of negotiations. It was not immediately apparent, but the Nez Perce had inflicted the eventual causes of their own defeat upon themselves. In the hasty evacuation of their village, much of their food and warm clothing was left behind – which would seriously degrade their ability to fight a protracted campaign.

PURSUIT (JULY–AUGUST 1877)

Go in and strike them hard!
Second Lieutenant Charles Woodruff at the Big Hole, August 10, 1877

UP THE LOLO TRAIL

After abandoning their village on the afternoon of July 12, the Nez Perce moved north toward Kamiah and began crossing to the north side of the middle branch of the Clearwater the next day. A small rearguard under Ollokot was left near the crossing site to delay any pursuing soldiers. The band leaders were uncertain what to do next and held a council near Weippe to decide their course of action. While they all agreed that ascending the Lolo Trail into Montana's Bitterroot Valley was the best method of shaking Howard's pursuit, they disagreed on their ultimate objective. Joseph still argued for returning circuitously to either his own Wallowa Valley or the Salmon River area, while White Bird advocated escaping to Canada and Looking Glass suggested moving into Montana's flat buffalo country and joining forces with the Crow tribe, who were supposedly friendly.

While the Nez Perce were debating their course of action, Howard followed their trail toward Kamiah, with Perry's cavalry in the lead. As they approached the river, Perry's cavalry ran into Ollokot's ambush and were driven off in disorder. By the time that Howard arrived at the river, all of the Nez Perce were across and his own troops could not immediately follow. He ordered his artillery to shell the distant Nez Perce, but no damage was done. Once again, the Nez Perce had outmaneuvered Howard and put a river between themselves and his pursuit. Howard's column camped on the south side of the river while awaiting boats, but on July 15 a Nez Perce messenger crossed the river to offer a parley. About 50 Nez Perce who were not part of the original outbreak agreed to surrender and go to the reservation, but Howard had them imprisoned at Fort Lapwai. These prisoners claimed that Joseph and many others were dispirited after the battle of the Clearwater and ready to discuss terms, but this parley was actually a diversion to conceal the fact that the Nez Perce were beginning to ascend the Lolo Trail.

Howard spent all of July 16 getting his column across the Clearwater and then dispatched his cavalry, McConville and his volunteers and some Christian Nez Perce scouts to probe up the trail. After moving about 20 miles (32km), the cavalry ran into another Nez Perce ambush in some thick woods, resulting in their scouts suffering three casualties. The demoralized 1st Cavalry detachment retreated precipitously to the Clearwater. Just prior to moving up the trail, the Non-Treaty Nez Perce proceeded to plunder food, horses and other supplies from Treaty Nez Perce in the area, whom they despised for submitting to

Nez Perce Trail, July–September 1877

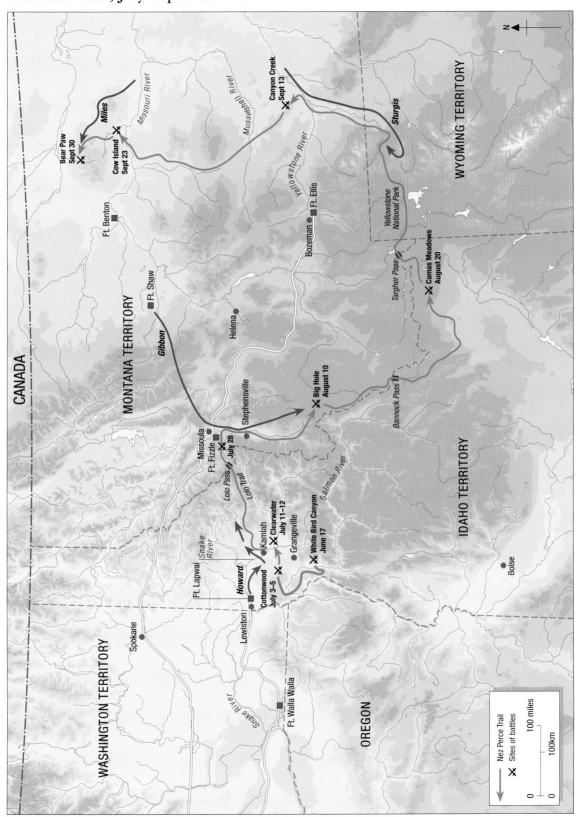

CANADA

Missouri River

Musselshell River

Yellowstone River

Miles

Bear Paw
Sept 30

Cow Island
Sept 23

Ft. Benton

Canyon Creek
Sept 13

Sturgis

WYOMING TERRITORY

MONTANA TERRITORY

Ft. Shaw

Ft. Ellis

Bozeman

Yellowstone National Park

Gibbon

Helena

Targhee Pass

Camas Meadows
August 20

Stephensville

Big Hole
August 10

Bannock Pass

Missoula
Ft. Fizzle // July 28

Lolo Trail
Lolo Pass

Salmon River

IDAHO TERRITORY

Kamiah

Clearwater
July 11–12

Grangeville

White Bird Canyon
June 17

Boise

Snake River

Ft. Lapwai   Howard

Cottonwood
July 3–5

Lewiston

Spokane

WASHINGTON TERRITORY

Snake River

Ft. Walla Walla

OREGON

Nez Perce Trail
✗ Sites of battles

0   100 miles
0   100km

55

Howard's troops encamped near Kamiah along the Clearwater River in mid-July 1877. Owing to poor planning, Howard brought along few tents, bridging material or rations, which hobbled his pursuit. While the Nez Perce were escaping up the Lolo Trail, Howard sat motionless for nearly three weeks here. (Author's collection)

reservation life. Apparently, blood was not thicker than water for the Nez Perce. On July 16, the Non-Treaty Nez Perce began their trek up the Lolo Trail and they reached the summit at Lolo Pass on July 22 – an average of better than 15 miles (24km) per day over mountainous terrain.

FORT FIZZLE

After his feeble effort at pursuit failed, Howard suspended operations for the next two weeks and focused on gathering more reinforcements and supplies for a protracted campaign. Given that his operations to date had been hindered by lack of troops and supplies, Howard intended to avoid further combat until he could guarantee a victory. By July 30, he had reorganized his column on the Clearwater that had been reinforced to 730 men, four pieces of artillery and 250 pack mules with supplies for 20 days. Colonel Frank Wheaton's 2nd Infantry had just arrived after a two-week trip from Atlanta and Howard ordered that regiment, plus two companies of cavalry, to head north to Coeur d'Alene then take the Mullan Road to meet him in Missoula. However, by taking the Lolo Trail into Montana, the Nez Perce were unwittingly complicating Howard's pursuit by crossing army jurisdictional boundaries. Montana lay within Brigadier-General Alfred H. Terry's Department of the Dakota, so Howard sent a request by telegraph to Terry to send a blocking force to delay the Nez Perce at the northern exit of the Lolo Trail. Unfortunately, Terry had not expected the Nez Perce campaign to spill over into his department and had few forces immediately available near the Lolo Trail. The only troops at hand were two companies of the 7th Infantry under Captain Charles C. Rawn at Missoula, augmented with some armed volunteers. Terry ordered Rawn to deploy scouts on the northern end of the

Lolo Trail to watch for the Nez Perce and to construct a fortified blocking position to delay them until Howard's force arrived. Terry also alerted Colonel John Gibbon, the district commander for western Montana, to prepare a column from his 7th Infantry for operations against the Nez Perce.

On the morning of June 25, Rawn moved his small detachment to a site 11 miles (18km) southwest of Missoula and began establishing his blocking position in a narrow, 1,200ft-wide (365m) valley with steep slopes. His troops had few tools other than their new trowel bayonets, so they were only able to dig shallow rile pits, topped by split logs. Rawn's men had just begun constructing their hasty earthworks when the main body of the Nez Perce arrived. Rawn met with Joseph and Looking Glass under a flag of truce, where he demanded that the Nez Perce disarm, but they indicated that they had no wish to fight soldiers or settlers in Montana and would pass through quietly if left unmolested. On July 27, Benjamin F. Potts, the Montana territorial governor, hurried to Missoula and joined in the negotiations. Rawn was in a difficult position; he knew that his mission was to delay the Nez Perce until Howard arrived, but realized that his 50 regulars and 150 armed volunteers were insufficient to disarm or defeat the Nez Perce. On the other hand, Potts and the civilian volunteers were willing to accept Nez Perce guarantees that their property would not be harmed if they gave free passage and were thus disinclined to mount a desperate and pointless defense. When the volunteers starting going home, Rawn was left with barely 60 men to hold the barricade. By this point, Looking Glass decided that Rawn's tiny force posed no threat and could simply be bypassed. On the night of July 28, the entire Nez Perce group, warriors, civilians and 2,000 ponies, climbed the ridgeline on Rawn's right and moved around his pathetic position on the high ground. Before he realized what was happening, the Nez Perce simply walked around Rawn and headed into Montana. Rawn's futile blocking position was soon dubbed "Fort Fizzle" for its utter failure to stop or delay the Nez Perce.

Advance Guard by Frederic Remington. In a pursuit operation, cavalry needs to maintain contact with the enemy but the 1st Cavalry consistently failed at this mission during the Nez Perce Campaign. (Library of Congress)

Two days after the Nez Perce bypassed Fort Fizzle, Howard finally resumed his pursuit and began ponderously moving up the Lolo Trail with his mixed 587-man command. It rained heavily, turning much of the narrow trail into thick mud. A group of Bannock scouts led by Buffalo Horn reconnoitered ahead of the main body, but many of these tribesmen were less than enthusiastic about their task. Civilian volunteers with axes cleared the path of trees felled by the retreating Nez Perce to delay the pursuit. Fortunately for Howard, the Nez Perce did not leave a stay-behind force to harass his main body. Howard – with no sense of security in Indian warfare – ordered a large bonfire to be lit in front of his command tent every night, which could have made him an excellent target for any Nez Perce marksmen lurking in the woods. Howard finally crossed the Lolo Pass in early August and received a courier from Gibbon informing him about his pursuit of the Nez Perce down the Bitterroot Valley. Howard decided to leave the bulk of his command behind and press on with the 221 men of Major George Sanford's battalion of the 1st Cavalry to support Gibbon.

BATTLE OF THE BIG HOLE

Once in the Bitterroot Valley, the Nez Perce headed south. Despite Governor Potts's declaration that, "the Indian murderers must not pass unmolested," his efforts to organize another volunteer battalion to delay them came to nothing. Instead, the Nez Perce moved at a leisurely pace down the Bitterroot, moving only 28 miles (45km) in three days. On July 28, they reached the town of Stevensville, where Looking Glass told local shopkeepers that they would pay in gold for provisions but if refused, they would take what they wanted by force. Relations with the townspeople were strained, but the Nez Perce succeeded in purchasing some food and supplies. However, Nez Perce relations with the local Flathead tribe, led by Chief Charlot, were worse.

A replica of an entrenchment built at Fort Fizzle. Looking Glass contemptuously referred to the flimsy defenses as a "soldier corral." The Nez Perce easily bypassed these fieldworks on the ridgeline in the background. (Author's collection)

TOP
Looking toward the Nez Perce village at the Big Hole from Gibbon's initial attack position. The dense brush provided effective concealment, which allowed the soldiers to approach stealthily before dawn. (Author's collection)

BOTTOM
Three companies of the 7th Infantry charged across the waist-deep Big Hole River just before dawn and fired three volleys into the clustered Nez Perce lodges. (Author's collection)

Chief Charlot had already provided scouts to Rawn and rejected Nez Perce requests for aid and comfort. Upon hearing this, the Nez Perce warned the Flatheads to stay out of their way. Captain Rawn's scouts followed discreetly at a distance for several days, reporting on the progress of the Nez Perce down the Bitterroot. While moving down the Bitterroot Valley, 18 lodges of local Nez Perce renegades, including Poker Joe, joined their column. On August 7, the Nez Perce reached the North Fork of the Big Hole River at a site known as Iskumtselalik Pah (the place of the buffalo calf) which they had used in previous years en route to buffalo hunts in Montana, where they established a village with 89 lodges and paused to rest their people after the long march from Idaho. Looking Glass and the other chiefs believed that they were relatively safe here in this uninhabited area and settled into a peaceful mode, with little attention to local security.

TOP

After suffering heavy casualties in the battle for the village, Gibbon's men retreated back across the Big Hole River, moving from the left to the wooded knoll on the right. Gibbon's men were besieged there for over 24 hours. (Author's collection)

BOTTOM

A 12-pdr mountain howitzer pointed at the Nez Perce village. On the morning of the battle, the howitzer managed to lob only two unfused shells at the village before it was overrun and captured by the Nez Perce. (Author's collection)

Even before the Nez Perce bypassed "Fort Fizzle," Colonel John Gibbon had begun assembling companies from his dispersed 7th Infantry at Fort Ellis. Just as the Nez Perce were entering the Bitterroot Valley, Gibbon marched with three half-strength companies and reached Missoula on August 3. There, he incorporated Rawn's troops and formed a composite infantry battalion with a total of 161 men and one mountain howitzer. It was a puny force but Gibbon was determined to bring the Nez Perce to heel. In the afternoon of August 4, he began his pursuit down the Bitterroot, with his infantry loaded in wagons. An 11-man mounted detachment under Lieutenant James Bradley, augmented with 38 volunteers, scouted ahead of the main body and discovered the Nez Perce camp on the Big Hole River around 1700hrs on August 7. Bradley and his men remained quietly in position on August 8, scouting out the layout of the enemy camp, until Gibbon arrived with the main body just before sunset. Once informed of the enemy dispositions, Gibbon decided to rest his troops for a few hours and then at midnight, began moving an assault force of 159 soldiers and

34 volunteers stealthily to a wooded area within sight of the village. The troops carried only their rifles and 100 rounds of ammunition per man, leaving their rations and canteens at the logistic trains with a small guard force, 4 miles (6km) from the Nez Perce camp.

In the darkness, Gibbon's troops moved quietly in single file around a large, grassy hill and reached an area on the west side of the river adjacent to the Nez Perce village around 0200hrs and settled down to wait for sunrise. Tall willows and underbrush along the river provided concealment. Amazingly, the Nez Perce had not deployed any sentries around the village and were completely unaware of the arrival of the soldiers. Even worse, Gibbon's men were between the Nez Perce and their pony herd, which was left unattended on an open hillside. Before dawn, Gibbon deployed Companies D and K in

A highly unrealistic depiction of Gibbon's troops under siege at the Big Hole, which appeared in *Harper's Weekly* in December 1895. In fact, Gibbon's men spent most of their time in the siege area on their stomachs and anyone foolish enough to stand up to fire or issue orders was quickly shot down. Media coverage of the Nez Perce campaign was often careless with facts and helped to distort postwar perceptions. (Author's collection)

US ARMY
1 Armed volunteers (Bradley)
2 Company K, 7th Infantry (Sanno)
3 Company D, 7th Infantry (Comba)
4 Company G, 7th Infantry (Browning)
5 Company I, 7th Infantry (Rawn)
6 Company F, 7th Infantry (Williams)
7 Company A, 7th Infantry (Logan)
8 12-pdr mountain howitzer

NEZ PERCE
A Nez Perce village
B Nez Perce pony herd
C Chief Josef and a handful of warriors
D White Bird group
E Looking Glass group
F Small groups of Nez Perce snipers

NORTH FORK BIG HOLE RIVER

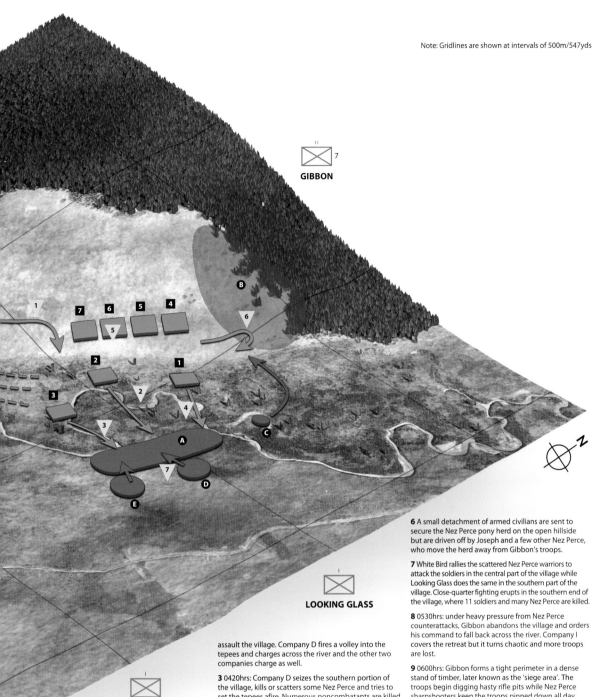

Note: Gridlines are shown at intervals of 500m/547yds

GIBBON

LOOKING GLASS

WHITE BIRD

EVENTS

1 0200hrs: Gibbon's command quietly arrives adjacent to the Nez Perce village and waits for sunrise. The Nez Perce fail to detect the arrival of the soldiers.

2 0400hrs: Gibbon orders Companies D and K and First Lieutenant Bradley's mixed force to advance in skirmish line across the North Fork of the Big Hole River and assault the village. Company D fires a volley into the tepees and charges across the river and the other two companies charge as well.

3 0420hrs: Company D seizes the southern portion of the village, kills or scatters some Nez Perce and tries to set the tepees afire. Numerous noncombatants are killed inside the tepees or as they try to flee.

4 Company K pauses outside the village to fire two volleys into the teepees, but loses momentum when two Nez Perce marksmen kill two soldiers. Meanwhile, Lt. Bradley is killed on the edge of the village and his leaderless force engages in protracted sniping with nearby Nez Perce from the willows.

5 Gibbon commits Companies A, F and I to support Company D on the right and Company G to support Company K in the center. He moves into the village but is wounded en route.

6 A small detachment of armed civilians are sent to secure the Nez Perce pony herd on the open hillside but are driven off by Joseph and a few other Nez Perce, who move the herd away from Gibbon's troops.

7 White Bird rallies the scattered Nez Perce warriors to attack the soldiers in the central part of the village while Looking Glass does the same in the southern part of the village. Close-quarter fighting erupts in the southern end of the village, where 11 soldiers and many Nez Perce are killed.

8 0530hrs: under heavy pressure from Nez Perce counterattacks, Gibbon abandons the village and orders his command to fall back across the river. Company I covers the retreat but it turns chaotic and more troops are lost.

9 0600hrs: Gibbon forms a tight perimeter in a dense stand of timber, later known as the 'siege area'. The troops begin digging hasty rifle pits while Nez Perce sharpshooters keep the troops pinned down all day.

10 The mountain howitzer arrives and lobs two shells into the southern edge of the village before the position is overrun by Yellow Wolf and five other Nez Perce. After dispersing the crew, the Nez Perce dismantle the howitzer.

11 In a final effort, the Nez Perce try to start a grass fire to burn the soldiers out of their fortified area, but this fails. While Looking Glass's warriors keep Gibbon's troops under fire in the siege area until nightfall, Joseph evacuates the survivors of the village eastward to escape before Howard arrives with reinforcements.

BATTLE OF THE BIG HOLE, AUGUST 9, 1877
The 7th Infantry's assault on the Nez Perce village ends in failure.

Indian warriors setting grass on fire, which was a common tactic. At the Big Hole, the Nez Perce set the grass on fire in an unsuccessful effort to burn Gibbon's men out of their siege area, but it may also have been intended to create a smokescreen to conceal the movement of their noncombatants away from the battlefield. (Author's collection)

skirmish line formation, along with Lt. Bradley's detachment and at 0400hrs as the top of the tepees became discernable he ordered them to cross the river and assault the village. As they advanced through the thick reeds on the river bottom, Bradley's detachment bumped into an elderly Indian who was going to attend to the pony herd. A volunteer fired at this Indian and killed him, but the shot alerted the village. With surprise gone, the infantry bolted across the hip-deep river and began firing three volleys into the tepees, as ordered by Gibbon. For the first time in the war, the Nez Perce were caught totally by surprise and the violence of the early morning assault stunned them. Even worse, either by luck or as a result of Lt. Bradley's pre-battle surveillance, Gibbon's main effort struck into the area where all five Non-Treaty band leaders had their lodges. The initial volleys killed or wounded a large number of Nez Perce, including Hahtalekin, leader of the Palouse band, but also hit women and children. In the early morning darkness, the soldiers could not distinguish between combatants and noncombatants and simply fired on anything that came out of the tepees. Many of the warriors simply abandoned their families and ran off eastward, away from the soldiers. Within 20 minutes, Company D had seized the southern portion of the village and began setting some tepees alight. All told, eight of 89 tepees were burned.

On the left flank, the soldiers encountered tougher resistance. Lt. Bradley was killed in the first moments of the action and Company K suffered two dead, which caused these units to stop outside the northern end of the village and engage in a protracted firefight. Captain Sanno's Company K appears to have been particularly indiscriminate and killed at least 11 women and children inside tepees. Sensing victory, Gibbon committed his four remaining companies to support the attack, but en route to the village his horse was killed and he was shot in the thigh. Gibbon made his first mistake by leaving no reserve and his second when he delegated the seizure of the unguarded pony herd to the civilian volunteers, whom he held in contempt. What should have been his main effort ended up as a half-hearted attempt to seize the ponies and when Joseph arrived with a few warriors, the volunteers were easily driven off. After the initial shock of the soldiers' attack wore off, Looking Glass, White Bird, Ollokot and others were able to rally the warriors and led them in a furious counterattack back into the village that resulted in a half-hour-long close-quarter battle. Losses were heavy on both sides, but when Captain William Logan and ten other soldiers were killed, Gibbon decided to abandon the village and retreat back across the river to a wooded knoll. Without a reserve to cover their withdrawal, the retreat became a disorganized stampede across the waterlogged lowland and the wooded knoll offered little sanctuary. As the infantry formed a tight little perimeter and began digging hasty rifle pits with their trowel bayonets, the Nez Perce began to swarm around them and pepper them with accurate rifle fire. Gibbon's troops were pinned down and outnumbered by an enemy on higher ground – a very poor tactical position. Nor could they count on any fire support, since the Nez Perce swarmed up a nearby hill and captured the mountain howitzer after it fired only two ineffectual rounds at the village. In their haste, the gunners had failed to insert the fuses in the shells. The Nez Perce also captured the pack mules, with their precious cargo of 2,000 rounds of rifle ammunition.

The Nez Perce kept Gibbon's men under constant pressure while their village began preparations to move out, including trying to burn the soldiers out with a grass fire. However, the Nez Perce knew that more soldiers were coming and while Looking Glass and his warriors kept Gibbon pinned down, Joseph spent the day moving the noncombatants out to the east. The battle of the Big Hole was a shock for the Nez Perce since they had believed that the campaign was over and the scale of the losses suffered in just two hours of fighting was catastrophic for a small tribe. Approximately 60 Nez Perce – 30 warriors and 30 noncombatants – were killed in the battle and at least 18 wounded, meaning a total loss of about ten percent. Both Shore Crossing and Red Moccasin Tops – the instigators of the war – were among the dead. Gibbon's troops had also been roughly handled, with 31 killed and 38 wounded. Indeed, Gibbon's troops could do little but remain in their fortified perimeter and bleed until Howard arrived with his advance guard of 20 cavalrymen at 1000hrs on August 11. Gibbon's troops had not eaten in three days and his wounded were in very poor shape, so the 7th Infantry was effectively out of the campaign.

Indian accounts of the battle of the Big Hole refer to it as a massacre and cite indiscriminate shooting of noncombatants as proof. However, there was absolutely no way for Gibbon's soldiers to discriminate between Indian combatants and noncombatants when they were all mixed together in one village. While some soldiers did deliberately kill noncombatants at the Big Hole, there is also no doubt that Nez Perce women and young boys also took part in the fighting and inflicted casualties upon the US Army. Furthermore, Gibbon ensured that some of the captured noncombatants were unharmed or released, whereas once again, the Nez Perce killed any wounded soldiers left in the village. Indeed, it was Gibbon's trapped command, having suffered 35 percent losses, that was in danger of annihilation until relieved by Howard. Yet the damage inflicted on the Nez Perce at the Big Hole was serious and undermined their morale by demonstrating that there would be no rest for them in Montana.

CAMAS MEADOWS

After the battle of the Big Hole, the Nez Perce marched southward, intent upon putting as much distance as possible between themselves and Howard's pursuit force. Having been proven wrong about the safety afforded by the Bitterroot Valley, Looking Glass lost much of his prestige after the Big Hole and Poker Joe, who was more familiar with the local area, directed the march southward. The Nez Perce also abandoned their 'do-no-harm' policy after the battle and began to attack local settlers they came across, killing five men on August 12 and another five on August 15. Farms were burned and horses were stolen, causing local communities to appeal to the US Army to stop the raids. Having finally ascended the Lolo Pass into Montana, Howard was following about two days behind the Nez Perce, but his column was spread out over a very large area and his vanguard consisted primarily of Major George Sanford's battalion of the 1st Cavalry. A small number of friendly Bannock scouts probed ahead, looking for the Nez Perce. Most of Howard's infantry and artillery lagged 20–40 (32–64km) miles behind.

Poker Joe led the Nez Perce through the Bannock Pass back into Idaho on August 13 and they began a slow circuitous loop to the southeast, keeping the mountains between themselves and their pursuers. Howard decided not to follow them directly but to try and get ahead with his cavalry and by the evening of August 18, his scouts discovered that the Nez Perce were less than 20 miles (32km) distant. The next evening, Howard's command camped at Camas Meadows, which offered good grazing for the tired horses and he hoped that, once rested, they could catch up with the fleeing Nez Perce.

A Friend in Need by Western artist Charles Schreyvogel. Care and maintenance of horses was critical in a sustained pursuit operation but virtually all the cavalry companies in the campaign were driven to the point where they were virtually combat ineffective. (Library of Congress)

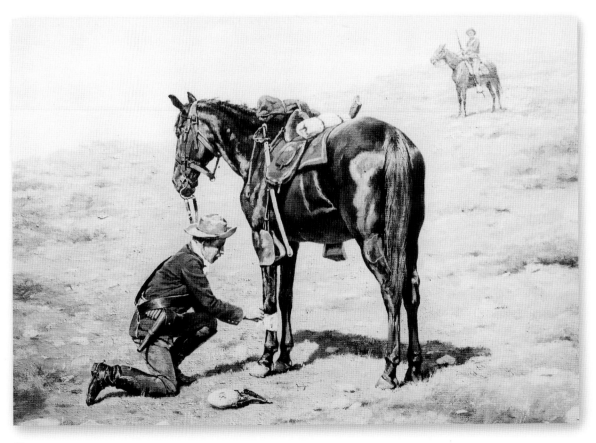

Instead, realizing that only a small portion of Howard's column was at Camas Meadows, the Nez Perce decided to conduct a spoiling attack of their own. A large mounted force of Nez Perce led by Looking Glass and Ollokot approached Howard's perimeter around 0330hrs on August 20, which panicked the 40 civilian volunteers. Although Company H, 8th Infantry, had pickets deployed much of the camp was in a relaxed state and the Nez Perce were able to get into the perimeter and capture about 150 pack mules before the soldiers could react. Howard angrily ordered Maj. Sanford to pursue the Nez Perce and retrieve the pack mules, so at sunup Companies B and I of the 1st Cavalry and L of the 2nd Cavalry set out after the enemy. About 6 miles (10km) east of Howard's camp, Sanford's cavalry succeeded in recapturing a few mules but ran straight into a Nez Perce ambush near a rocky outcrop. The cavalry deployed in skirmish line and fired back for about 20 minutes, suffering one killed, before they realized that the Nez Perce outnumbered them and had better cover, so they withdrew in haste.

While trying to break contact, Company L of the 2nd Cavalry, led by Captain Randolph Norwood, became separated from the other two companies and was forced to dismount and build breastworks. The Nez Perce swarmed around this isolated company in an effort to annihilate it and a nasty fight ensued. Norwood's company suffered eight casualties but managed to kill six warriors – an unusually high casualty rate for the Nez Perce. Sanford failed to support Norwood until Howard marched out with his infantry and together they relieved Norwood and the Nez Perce retired. Although it had been an expensive raid, Looking Glass succeeded in capturing enough of Howard's pack train to impede the pursuit.

Once the main body of infantry arrived at Camas Meadows, Howard returned to the pursuit on August 21 but after three days of fruitless marching he came to a halt near Henrys Lake. Both supplies and morale were very low and the cavalry mounts worn out, meaning that further pursuit over rough terrain was out of the question. Howard decided temporarily to suspend the pursuit and rest his tired command near the lake for four days, while sending for more supplies and pack mules. He also was able to send a telegraph message to Gen. William Sherman, who was at Fort Shaw in Montana. When Howard complained that his column was worn out, Sherman replied that "if you are tired, give the command to some young energetic officer" and that the forces in Terry's department could deal with the Nez Perce. Howard bristled at the possibility of turning over an unsuccessful campaign to anyone else, which would reflect poorly on him, so he immediately informed Sherman that he would recommence the pursuit. Increasingly, even the troops began to realize that the pursuit was being impelled by Howard's personal agenda rather than military logic.

YELLOWSTONE

The United States Congress had created the Yellowstone National Park in 1872, a rectangular area of over 3,000 square miles (7,770 square kilometers) in northwest Wyoming. There were no towns or roads and very few Indians in this uninhabited wilderness area, which initially fell under the jurisdiction of the US Army. On August 23, the Nez Perce crossed the Targhee (Tacher) Pass, 5 miles (8km) east of Henrys Lake, which offered direct access into the west side of Yellowstone. The next day, the Nez Perce bumped into a small

Outmaneuvering the 7th Cavalry in Yellowstone, September 5–11, 1877

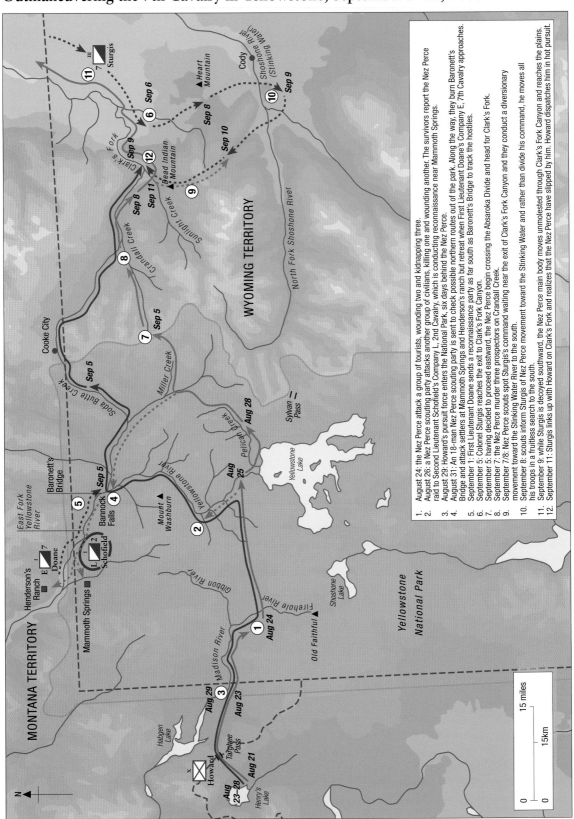

1. August 24: the Nez Perce attack a group of tourists, wounding three.
2. August 26: a Nez Perce scouting party attacks another group of civilians, killing one and wounding another. The survivors report the Nez Perce raid to Second Lieutenant Schofield's Company L, 2nd Cavalry, which is conducting reconnaissance near Mammoth Springs.
3. August 29: Howard's pursuit force enters the National Park, six days behind the Nez Perce.
4. August 31: An 18-man Nez Perce scouting party is sent to check possible northern routes out of the park. Along the way, they burn Baronett's Bridge and attack settlers at Mammoth Springs and Henderson's ranch but retreat when First Lieutenant Doane's Company E, 7th Cavalry approaches.
5. September 1: First Lieutenant Doane sends a reconnaissance party as far south as Baronett's Bridge to track the hostiles.
6. September 5: Colonel Sturgis reaches the exit to Clark's Fork Canyon.
7. September 5: having decided to proceed eastward, the Nez Perce begin crossing the Absaroka Divide and head for Clark's Fork.
8. September 7: the Nez Perce murder three prospectors on Crandall Creek.
9. September 7/8: Nez Perce scouts spot Sturgis's command waiting near the exit of Clark's Fork Canyon and they conduct a diversionary movement toward the Stinking Water River to the south.
10. September 8: scouts inform Sturgis of Nez Perce movement toward the Stinking Water and rather than divide his command, he moves all his troops in a fruitless search to the south.
11. September 9: while Sturgis is decoyed southward, the Nez Perce main body moves unmolested through Clark's Fork Canyon and reaches the plains.
12. September 11: Sturgis links up with Howard on Clark's Fork and realizes that the Nez Perce have slipped him. Howard dispatches him in hot pursuit.

Scare in a Pack Train by Frederic Remington. Here the artist effectively captures the gloom and isolation of night warfare on the plains. The Nez Perce raid on Howard's pack train at Camas Meadows precipitated a panic that cost him nearly a third of his supplies. (Author's collection)

group of tourists, murdering one and kidnapping the others. Normally, the Nez Perce did not take prisoners but they were far from home and unfamiliar with the Yellowstone Park, so they pressed a captured American prospector into service as a guide. Yellow Wolf led attacks on other civilians, killing one more and wounding two and rationalized the murders by saying that, "all white people seemed our enemy."

The Nez Perce march through the nearly trackless Yellowstone was brutal and took a great toll on the noncombatants and the pony herd, which had to be dragged across the Yellowstone River and up mountainous terrain. Those too weak to continue were left behind. Although the Nez Perce continued to head eastward to Yellowstone Lake, they were unsure whether they should exit the park to the east or try a northern route. In order to make an informed choice, scouting parties were sent out in several directions to check possible routes, while the main body rested along Pelican Creek for a few days. One 18-man party made it all the way to Mammoth Hot Springs and burned Henderson's Ranch.

While the Nez Perce made their way through the park, Howard sent 40 Bannock scouts under the civilian scout Stanton Fisher to track them. The Bannocks were able to follow the Nez Perce trail and report back to Howard, but there was no real chance of stopping the Nez Perce in Yellowstone. Instead, the Bannocks satisfied themselves with killing any weak or elderly Nez Perce left behind on the trail. Howard's main column plodded through the park, fully five–six days behind the Nez Perce. Sherman believed that Howard no longer had any chance of catching the Nez Perce and tried to cut him out of the campaign by sending a junior officer to take charge, but the replacement officer was unable to link up with Howard's column in Yellowstone. Sherman was also bitter that the Nez Perce had eluded capture for so long and telegrammed General Philip Sheridan, commander of the Division of the Missouri that: "If the Nez Perces be captured or surrender it should be without

Infantrymen in Yellowstone National Park soon after the Nez Perce War. It was difficult to move supply wagons through the trackless wilderness and troops could easily become disoriented. (National Archives)

terms. Their horses, arms and property should be taken away. Many of their leaders [should be] executed and preferably by sentence of a civil court for their murders in Idaho and Montana and what are left should be treated like the Modocs, sent to some other country; there should be extreme severity, else other tribes alike situated may imitate their example."

Sherman had lost faith in Howard's ability to stop the Nez Perce and even before they entered Yellowstone, he sent orders to Colonel Nelson A. Miles at the Tongue River cantonment to be prepared to take the field against the Nez Perce. Sherman knew that Miles was aggressive and energetic, as well as ambitious, and that his troops were seasoned veterans. Miles quickly dispatched First Lieutenant Gustavus Doane's Company E, 7th Cavalry, and 60 Crow scouts to reconnoiter the northern exits of Yellowstone, in case the Nez Perce moved back into Montana. In mid-August, Miles sent Colonel Samuel D. Sturgis with six more companies of the 7th Cavalry to be in position to act in case Doane spotted the Nez Perce. In fact, Doane's troops encountered a Nez Perce scouting party at Henderson's Ranch on August 31 and actively pursued them. Meanwhile, since he was ordered by Sherman to coordinate with Mile's forces, Howard tried to get several couriers to Sturgis to update him on Nez Perce movements, but the couriers failed to get through. However, Sturgis was aware that there were two likely routes for the Nez Perce to exit Yellowstone if they continued eastward – either northeast toward Clark's Fork Canyon or southeast through the Absaroka Mountains to the Stinking Water (later Shoshone) River.

By September 7, Sturgis had moved his 360-man command to Heart Mountain, which placed him in an excellent position to observe either eastward exit of the Yellowstone. Unfortunately at this critical point, Sturgis lost contact with both Doane's reconnaissance group and Howard's approaching column. After the Nez Perce became aware that Doane's company was watching the northern exit, they decided on September 5 to head east over the back-breaking Absaroka Divide and then toward Clark's Fork of the Yellowstone. Along the way, the Nez Perce murdered four prospectors they encountered on Crandall Creek. The Nez Perce intended to use Clark's Fork Canyon but their scouts spotted Sturgis's command encamped not far from the exit. Cunningly, the Nez Perce sent several groups of mounted warriors southward toward the Stinking Water River and allowed themselves to be deliberately spotted by local civilians. When informed by the civilians of the Nez Perce activity near the Stinking Water, Sturgis made the poor decision to commit his entire force toward blocking the southern route and left nothing to cover Clark's Fork Canyon. Sturgis's decision was almost certainly caused by the apprehension within the 7th Cavalry about splitting the regiment in the face of the enemy after what had happened to Custer the year before. Taking no chances, Sturgis proceeded south after the Nez Perce diversionary force and spent two days following false leads. Once Sturgis was out of position, the Nez Perce main body moved through the narrow Clark's Fork Canyon unopposed and proceeded onto the flat plains. Had Sturgis left even a few companies at Clark's Fork Canyon, the Nez Perce would have probably suffered appalling losses in trying to break through this narrow choke point.

By the time that Sturgis became aware that he had been outmaneuvered, the Nez Perce were already heading north into the flat buffalo country of Montana. A crestfallen Sturgis linked up with Howard on September 11. Howard was incensed that Sturgis had missed his opportunity and duly ordered him to force-march after the fleeing Nez Perce. Shortly after leaving Yellowstone, the Nez Perce sent envoys to the Crows and found out that they would not receive any support from them. In fact, the Crows were providing scouts to the US Army and adopted a hostile attitude toward the Nez Perce. Now there was no hope of finding a sanctuary anywhere within the United States and the Nez Perce headed north toward their only hope – refuge with Sitting Bull in Canada.

Canyon Creek, September 13, 1877

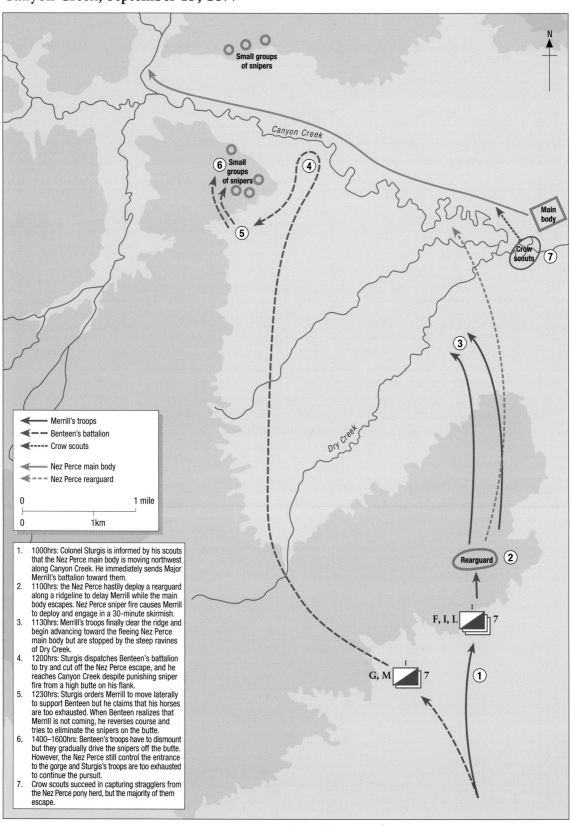

Legend:
- Merrill's troops
- Benteen's battalion
- Crow scouts
- Nez Perce main body
- Nez Perce rearguard

0 ————— 1 mile
0 ————— 1km

Map labels: N, Canyon Creek, Dry Creek, Small groups of snipers, Main body, Crow scouts, Rearguard, F, I, L, G, M

1. 1000hrs: Colonel Sturgis is informed by his scouts that the Nez Perce main body is moving northwest along Canyon Creek. He immediately sends Major Merrill's battalion toward them.
2. 1100hrs: the Nez Perce hastily deploy a rearguard along a ridgeline to delay Merrill while the main body escapes. Nez Perce sniper fire causes Merrill to deploy and engage in a 30-minute skirmish.
3. 1130hrs: Merrill's troops finally clear the ridge and begin advancing toward the fleeing Nez Perce main body but are stopped by the steep ravines of Dry Creek.
4. 1200hrs: Sturgis dispatches Benteen's battalion to try and cut off the Nez Perce escape, and he reaches Canyon Creek despite punishing sniper fire from a high butte on his flank.
5. 1230hrs: Sturgis orders Merrill to move laterally to support Benteen but he claims that his horses are too exhausted. When Benteen realizes that Merrill is not coming, he reverses course and tries to eliminate the snipers on the butte.
6. 1400–1600hrs: Benteen's troops have to dismount but they gradually drive the snipers off the butte. However, the Nez Perce still control the entrance to the gorge and Sturgis's troops are too exhausted to continue the pursuit.
7. Crow scouts succeed in capturing stragglers from the Nez Perce pony herd, but the majority of them escape.

THE ENDGAME (SEPTEMBER 1877)

There should be extreme severity
General William Sherman, August 31, 1877

CANYON CREEK

At 0500hrs on September 12, Sturgis set off with the 7th Cavalry divided into two battalions: Major Lewis Merrill's battalion (Companies F, I and L) and Captain Frederick W. Benteen's battalion (Companies G and M). Sturgis's column spent an incredible 18 hours in the saddle that day and marched over 60 miles (100km), which thoroughly exhausted their horses but brought the 7th Cavalry hard up on the heels of the Nez Perce. That same day, the Nez Perce crossed to the north side of the Yellowstone and began foraging for supplies, which brought them into conflict with local settlers. The Nez Perce murdered two settlers and burned several houses.

Miles mounted his 5th Infantry on captured Sioux ponies so they could keep up with the 7th Cavalry and intercept the Nez Perce before they reached Canada. (Author's collection)

Sturgis's column began crossing the Yellowstone River at 1000hrs the next morning and was soon informed by their Crow scouts that the Nez Perce were nearby. Sturgis immediately moved Merrill's battalion toward the enemy, with Benteen following. The Nez Perce were equally surprised at the sudden appearance of soldiers – they had neglected to deploy any scouts to watch their rear since Howard's cavalry had never moved so fast – and now tried to usher their noncombatants and pony herd westward along Canyon Creek to escape the approaching 7th Cavalry. The Nez Perce managed to deploy a small mounted rearguard on a ridge between the cavalry and their retreating tribe and these snipers forced Merrill to deploy his three companies into a mounted skirmish line. Rather than closing the distance and eliminating the small rearguard, Merrill was satisfied with a useless 30-minute firefight with the Nez Perce at a distance well beyond effective carbine range. By the time that Merrill's men had cleared the ridge, the main body of Nez Perce were vanishing in the distance.

Sturgis reached the ridge and realized that there was still a chance to cut off the Nez Perce pony herd at a narrow, steep canyon to the northeast and he ordered Benteen to advance rapidly to seize the key terrain. In the best tradition of the 7th Cavalry, Benteen moved intrepidly toward the bottleneck, receiving Nez Perce sniper fire that inflicted five casualties, but driving on. Benteen might have captured part of the pony herd, but Merrill failed to support him, claiming that his troops and horses were too exhausted to move out. Realizing that he was approaching a much larger enemy force with just two weak companies and not intending to repeat the disaster at the Little Bighorn, Benteen veered off and rejoined the rest of Sturgis's command. However, the Crow scouts – who took no active part in the fighting – succeeded in capturing some stragglers from the Nez Perce pony herd.

The 7th Cavalry suffered four dead and seven wounded at the battle of Canyon Creek, against one dead and three wounded for the Nez Perce. Although Sturgis failed to defeat the Nez Perce, they had lost some horses, which reduced their mobility a bit, and they were shocked that the cavalry was able to catch up with them. Sturgis's force went into battle too tired to maneuver effectively, which reduced their ability to close with the enemy.

Indian scouts disguised as buffalo. While the Nez Perce warriors had plenty of battlefield cunning, they often proved sloppy at reconnaissance and were caught by surprise repeatedly. (Author's collection)

Nevertheless, the action at Canyon Creek was the beginning of the endgame against the Nez Perce, with the Indians losing their lead and new forces gathering in their path.

THE BUFFALO COUNTRY

Sturgis continued his pursuit for two more days and reached the Musselshell River by September 15, but the forced marches had virtually destroyed his horses. Almost 100 horses had been lost in just four days and one-third of his men were afoot. Supply arrangements had collapsed, leaving his men without rations for days, so Sturgis decided to give up the pursuit. However, he dispatched a large number of Crows after the Nez Perce and they succeeded in catching up and harassing the tribe for several days. While the Crows lacked the skill to stop the Nez Perce, they were adept at culling dozens of ponies from their herd and killing some of the noncombatant stragglers. These pinprick attacks were disheartening for the Nez Perce, since they indicated that not only Americans but even the local Indian tribes were hostile to them. In addition to losing more horses, the Nez Perce were also running dangerously low on ammunition in fending off constant attacks.

Howard finally caught up with the immobilized 7th Cavalry on September 21 and, after receiving fresh supplies, they set off together in slow pursuit northward. However, both Howard's and Sturgis's troops were spent and they realized that they could not catch the Nez Perce before they reached Canada. Howard was also aware that Colonel Miles was marching his own column to intercept the Nez Perce and resolved to do what he could to

The decisive moment in any US Army operation against hostile Indians was the capture of their pony herd, without which they were immobilized. However, the pursuing US troops did not come close to capturing the Nez Perce herd and the action at Canyon Creek and did not succeed until Bear Paw. (Library of Congress)

THE 7TH CAVALRY'S CHARGE AT BEAR PAW MOUNTAIN, SEPTEMBER 30, 1877 (pp. 76–77)

By the morning of September 30, the Nez Perce believed that they had left their pursuers far behind and were now only about 40 miles (65km) from sanctuary in Canada. However, most of the Nez Perce were exhausted after three months of running and fighting and they paused to rest on the east bank of the Snake Creek, near Bear Paw Mountain. It was here that Colonel Nelson A. Miles caught them by surprise and he ordered the three companies of the 7th Cavalry under Captain Owen Hale (1) to mount an immediate charge to overrun the village before the warriors could react.

Hale led Companies A, D and K (2) across a narrow, flat-topped bluff while the 2nd Cavalry moved to outflank the village and capture the Nez Perce pony herd. As they charged toward the village, Nez Perce warriors began to fire upon the cavalry and Hale's 44-man Company K veered toward the right and became separated from the other two companies. Just as the mounted troopers approached the edge of the bluff, Yellow Wolf and about 20 warriors (3) emerged and poured a devastating point-blank fire into Company K, emptying several saddles and halting the charge. Hale ordered his men to dismount and form a skirmish line but soon found themselves isolated and under fire from three directions. An intense firefight follows, with half of Company K's men killed or wounded, but Nez Perce casualties are also heavy. With ammunition running low, Captain Hale was killed when shot in the neck and the survivors broke and ran back toward the position held by the rest of Miles's command.

support his former protégé. All of the 1st Cavalry units were sent back to their home stations and Howard's remaining force was pared down to a more logistically sustainable column.

Meanwhile, the Nez Perce continued their march to Canada and took time out to raid some Crow villages in retaliation for their cooperation with the US Army. On the afternoon of September 23, the Nez Perce arrived at the army supply depot at Cow Island on the Missouri River. The well-stocked depot was guarded by 12 soldiers from Company B, 7th Infantry, who had fortified their outpost with boxes. Initially, the Nez Perce begged the soldiers for food but when that failed, they launched a night assault on the depot. Although the Nez Perce succeeded in capturing some food and supplies, some of their young warriors recklessly set a large store of bacon alight, which aided the soldiers in shooting at them and frustrated the attack. After an all-night siege of the depot, the Nez Perce marched off northward toward the Canadian border. On September 25, the Nez Perce encountered and sacked a wagon train they encountered at Cow Creek Canyon, 10 miles (16km) north of the Missouri River. A small force of armed volunteers engaged the Nez Perce near the wagon train in an inconclusive two-hour skirmish.

Fatigue and hunger were beginning to rob the Nez Perce of the initiative and after crossing the Missouri they began to slow down. Their leaders believed that Howard and Sturgis were too far behind to catch them – which was correct – and that they could slow down a bit to rest their people and horses. The nighttime temperatures were beginning to drop and the noncombatants could not survive long in the open once the snow came, so it was imperative to fashion new lodge poles. Reasserting command, Looking Glass decided that they should establish a camp on Snake Creek near Bear Paw Mountain on September 29. Since firewood was scarce on the flat plain, dried buffalo dung was used for their campfires, which prompted the Nez Perce to call this spot "Place of the Manure Fire." After a few days rest, Looking Glass reasoned that the Nez Perce could complete the final 40-mile (65km) leg to the Canadian border. Looking Glass's plan was reasonable, but did not take into account Colonel Nelson A Miles.

Captain Owen Hale, led the battalion of the 7th Cavalry in the attack on the Nez Perce village on the chilly morning of 30 September 1877. Hale and Company K were shot to pieces and the 7th Cavalry lost all three company commanders in less than 30 minutes of combat. (Author's collection)

BEAR PAW

Miles had received a message from Howard at the Tongue River cantonment on the evening of September 17 which alerted him to the fact that the Nez Perce had slipped by Sturgis and were heading north toward a possible link-up with the Sioux. Wasting no time, Miles assembled a 520-man mobile strike force consisting of a battalion from the 2nd Cavalry, a battalion from the 7th Cavalry and a battalion of his own 5th Infantry, as well as two artillery pieces and 36 supply wagons. The infantrymen were mounted on ponies recently captured from the Sioux and Miles intended to make good use of 30 cooperative Cheyenne as scouts. Setting out on September 18, Miles headed northwest toward the Missouri River, hoping to intercept the Nez Perce before they reached that obstacle. The column marched 146 miles (235km) across the prairie in six days and was ferried across the Missouri River by a steamboat on September 24–25.

Upon crossing the river, Miles learned about the Nez Perce attack upon the depot at Cow Island the day before. Realizing that the Nez Perce had already crossed the river and were probably well on their way to the

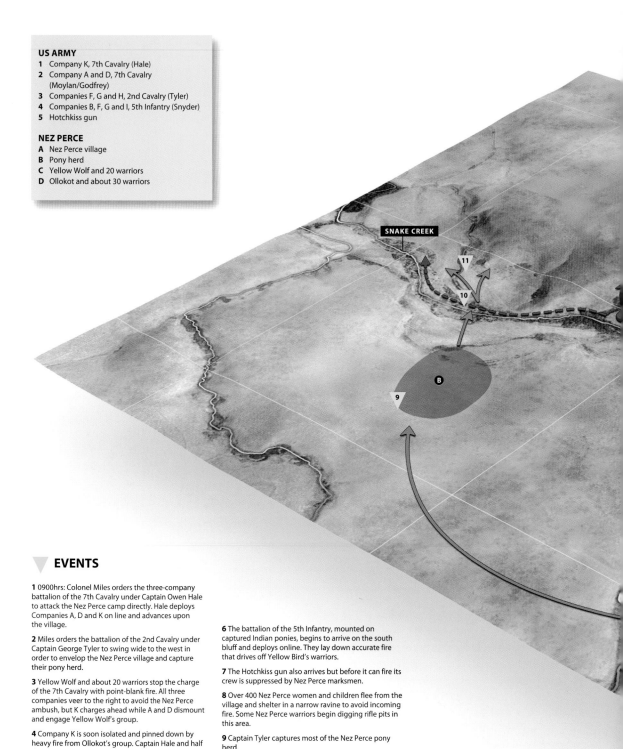

US ARMY
1 Company K, 7th Cavalry (Hale)
2 Company A and D, 7th Cavalry (Moylan/Godfrey)
3 Companies F, G and H, 2nd Cavalry (Tyler)
4 Companies B, F, G and I, 5th Infantry (Snyder)
5 Hotchkiss gun

NEZ PERCE
A Nez Perce village
B Pony herd
C Yellow Wolf and 20 warriors
D Ollokot and about 30 warriors

SNAKE CREEK

▼ **EVENTS**

1 0900hrs: Colonel Miles orders the three-company battalion of the 7th Cavalry under Captain Owen Hale to attack the Nez Perce camp directly. Hale deploys Companies A, D and K on line and advances upon the village.

2 Miles orders the battalion of the 2nd Cavalry under Captain George Tyler to swing wide to the west in order to envelop the Nez Perce village and capture their pony herd.

3 Yellow Wolf and about 20 warriors stop the charge of the 7th Cavalry with point-blank fire. All three companies veer to the right to avoid the Nez Perce ambush, but K charges ahead while A and D dismount and engage Yellow Wolf's group.

4 Company K is soon isolated and pinned down by heavy fire from Ollokot's group. Captain Hale and half the troop are killed or wounded. However, Ollokot is also killed.

5 Companies A and D move some troops forward to assist Company K but take heavy casualties. The remnants of K fall back with these troops toward the south bluff.

6 The battalion of the 5th Infantry, mounted on captured Indian ponies, begins to arrive on the south bluff and deploys online. They lay down accurate fire that drives off Yellow Bird's warriors.

7 The Hotchkiss gun also arrives but before it can fire its crew is suppressed by Nez Perce marksmen.

8 Over 400 Nez Perce women and children flee from the village and shelter in a narrow ravine to avoid incoming fire. Some Nez Perce warriors begin digging rifle pits in this area.

9 Captain Tyler captures most of the Nez Perce pony herd.

10 Company G, 2nd Cavalry, pursues a number of villagers who are fleeing up Snake Creek.

11 About 1200hrs: Chief Toohoolhoolzote and five other Nez Perce warriors are caught in the open near the Point of Rocks and killed by Company G.

BATTLE OF BEAR PAW, MORNING SEPTEMBER 30, 1877
The final encounter between the US and the Nez Perce forces.

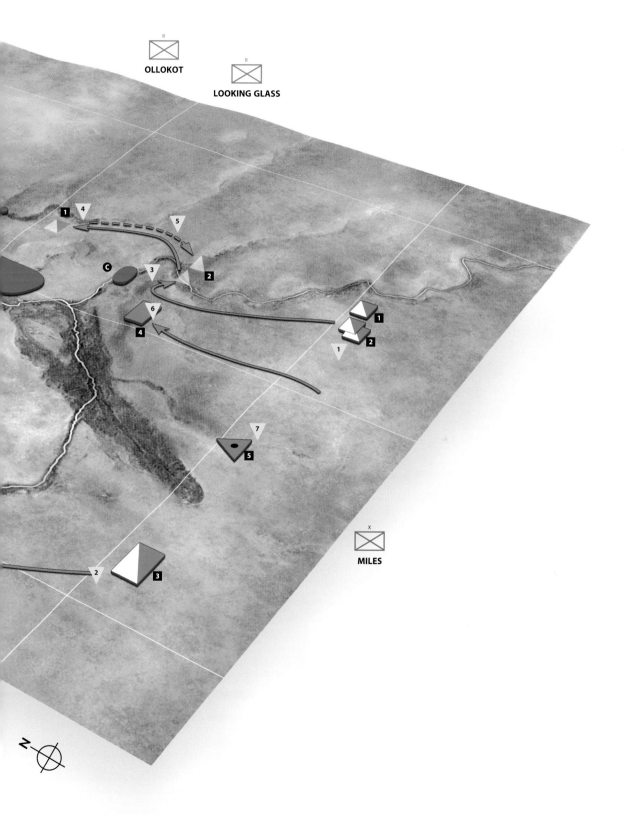

OLLOKOT

LOOKING GLASS

MILES

Captain Hale led Company K in a charge across this flat ridge toward the Nez Perce village. However, his troops soon were caught in a vicious crossfire from both sides as Nez Perce marksmen rose up from the edge of the ridge. (Author's collection)

Canadian border, he reoriented his column and marched northward toward Bear Paw Mountain on September 26. He deployed a cloud of scouts in front and on the flanks of his column, searching for the enemy and employed tight security to conceal his own movements. In four days, Miles's column marched 93 miles (150km) and came within sight of Bear Paw Mountain on the evening of September 29, just as a light snowstorm began. Some of Miles's scouts ran into a few Nez Perce engaged in rounding up stray horses and engaged in a brief firefight before retiring. While Miles took this skirmish as an indication that the Nez Perce camp was nearby, the Nez Perce leadership decided that there was no imminent threat and failed to send out scouts to provide any early warning.

Miles roused his troops before dawn on September 30 and moved out at 0440hrs. Around 0820hrs, a Cheyenne scout spotted smoke from the Nez Perce village and soon confirmed its location. However, a few mounted Nez Perce spotted the Cheyenne scouts and rode back to alert the village. As Miles crested a rise south of where the Nez Perce village lay, he could see the pony herd off to the west and signs of activity, but not the village itself. When some of his scouts claimed that the Nez Perce were beginning to flee, around 0900hrs Miles decided to mount an immediate pincer attack on the village and the pony herd before they escaped to Canada. He ordered Captain Owen Hale's three-company battalion of the 7th Cavalry to attack the Nez Perce camp directly, while Captain George Tyler's battalion of the 2nd Cavalry swung west to go after the pony herd. The trailing battalion of the 5th Infantry and the artillery would come into action as soon as possible to support the attack on the village.

Miles's decision to launch a hasty attack bordered on the reckless since he was committing his forces piecemeal and with only a rough idea of enemy dispositions, but he was driven by the fear – as Custer had been – that the hostiles would slip away. Although the Nez Perce had about 200 warriors near the village, they were caught by surprise and only a handful was immediately available to repel the cavalry attack. Hale's troopers moved in rapidly with all three companies almost on line but as they approached a ravine short of the village, they ran into an ambush by Yellow Wolf and about

LEFT
This is the ravine where most of the Nez Perce noncombatants sheltered from gunfire for five days. Warriors dug a number of rifle pits to fortify the position from attack and Miles had no intention of risking another close-quarter fight like the Big Hole. (Author's collection)

BELOW
This is the view from the Nez Perce ravine toward the low ridge held by the 5th Infantry, which was well within range of their Springfield rifles. The Hotchkiss gun was emplaced on the knoll to the right. (Author's collection)

Looking from the 5th Infantry's position toward the Nez Perce ravine. The infantry mounted one futile attack across the open ground to the left which was repulsed with heavy losses. (Author's collection)

20 warriors. Yellow Wolf's group was outnumbered more than five to one, but they poured a point-blank fire into the advancing cavalrymen that forced Companies A and D to dismount and form a skirmish line. Hale veered his company toward the right, away from the ambush, and galloped across a flat, grassy ridge toward the village, barely 200 yards (180m) away. However, Ollokot had gathered another group of warriors in a ravine in front of the troopers and as Hale's men got within sight of the village, Ollokot's warriors rose up and poured a lethal fire into them. Hale's company was in a poor position, isolated from the rest of the 7th Cavalry and under close-range fire from three sides. Company K was literally shot to pieces in a matter of minutes, with Hale and about half his troops killed. Yet the 7th Cavalry fought back hard and when Ollokot raised his head to fire he was shot and killed and other warriors were hit, too. Seeing Hale's company hard pressed, the other two companies of the 7th Cavalry broke free from Yellow Wolf's ambush and succeeded in moving to the rescue of the battered Company K and, together, they fell back toward the approaching mounted infantry.

While the 7th Cavalry made its futile attack on the village, Tyler's 2nd Cavalry had more luck against the poorly protected Nez Perce pony herd. Again and again, the Nez Perce repeated the same cardinal mistakes: inadequate local security around their villages and failure to safeguard their pony herd adequately. Even though the pony herd was the Nez Perce center of gravity – providing them their operational mobility – they continually located it on the far side of a water obstacle and failed to place even a token guard force with it. With the Cheyenne scouts in the lead, Tyler's cavalry was able to reach and capture a substantial part of the herd before the Nez Perce could react. Although the 7th Cavalry's attack failed, it caused about 70 Nez Perce – including some warriors – to flee northward in an "every-man-for-himself" style, which made them vulnerable to the 2nd Cavalry that was now between them and Canada. Tyler sent his Company G to pursue the fleeing villagers up Snake Creek and they captured and killed a number of Nez Perce. Even the aged Chief Toohoolhoolzote – no longer full of fight – was caught in the open with five other warriors and killed by Company G. With two chiefs dead and the bulk of their horses gone, the Nez Perce tactical situation was rapidly deteriorating.

Miles deployed the 155 troops from the 5th Infantry on the south bluffs, facing the Nez Perce village, and they began to lay down a base of fire that drove off most of the Nez Perce skirmishers. With their village now exposed, over 400 noncombatants abandoned their lodges and crowded into a narrow ravine to avoid the incoming fire. Miles deployed his Hotchkiss gun on a knoll to fire into the ravine but Nez Perce snipers kept the crew pinned down. Nevertheless, by noon Miles knew that he had cornered the Nez Perce and he thought he could finish them off quickly. Once the 7th Cavalry battalion was reorganized under a surviving lieutenant, Miles ordered a coordinated attack on the Nez Perce in the ravine at 1500hrs. However, the Nez Perce were ready and they repulsed the cavalry with accurate fire and an attack by 30 infantrymen from the south bluffs was also repulsed after suffering eight more casualties. Miles now accepted that the Nez Perce were dug in too well for his small command to overrun without excessive casualties and he decided to lay siege to their position.

Both sides fortified their positions during the night and tended to their wounded. Some of the Nez Perce warriors began to dig rifle pits in the ravine, later dubbed "the siege area." The 2nd Cavalry moved onto the bluffs north of the Nez Perce ravine, completing their encirclement. A wintry mix of snow

The view from the Hotchkiss gun position toward the ravine. Initially the Nez Perce were able to keep the gun out of action but eventually, its persistent fire into the ravine would help to convince Joseph of the futility of continued resistance. (Author's collection)

and sleet began to fall, adding to the misery of the Nez Perce, who had few blankets and could not light fires within range of the infantry's Springfield rifles. It had been a costly day for Miles's command, with a total of 23 dead and 39 wounded. The 7th Cavalry was particularly hard hit, having suffered 47 casualties of 115 engaged or a 40 percent loss rate. Nez Perce losses were also heavy, including about 22 dead.

The next morning, with the snow continuing to fall, Cheyenne scouts approached the Nez Perce position and were able to arrange for a truce to bury the dead. On pretense of recovering dead soldiers from Hale's company, Second Lieutenant Lovell H. Jerome and some Cheyenne scouts moved forward to the ravine to identify the Nez Perce rifle pits and to gauge the condition of their warriors. Miles agreed to meet with Joseph, who was concerned about the plight of his noncombatants. Inside a tent behind the 5th Infantry's positions, Miles met with Joseph to discuss surrender but Joseph was thinking more in terms of acceding to Howard's original ultimatum to go to the reservation. Unsatisfied with how the negotiations were going, Miles decided to violate the truce and he had Joseph arrested. Unfortunately, Miles was unaware of Lieutenant Jerome's reconnaissance and the Nez Perce promptly seized the young lieutenant as a hostage. Both Joseph and Lieutenant Jerome were held prisoner all night and then exchanged under another flag of truce on the morning of October 2. An uneasy truce lasted the

An idealized illustration of Joseph's surrender with his iconic "I will fight no more forever" gesture. In fact, most of the bodies were removed in a truce days before the surrender and Joseph was disarmed once negotiations began. Furthermore, this popular image ignores the fact that many Nez Perce warriors did not surrender at all. (Author's collection)

rest of the day as Miles received a supply train and a 12-pdr howitzer. Inside the ravine, the Nez Perce realized that they lacked the strength to break out of the encirclement but were unwilling to consider surrender, so they just gritted their teeth and hoped for help from Sitting Bull in Canada. Throughout the siege, Sitting Bull was the wild card for both sides; the Nez Perce were counting on the Sioux to arrive and drive off Miles's troops and Miles was concerned that hostile Sioux could appear in force to break the siege. The specter of Little Bighorn influenced both sides at Bear Paw.

At 1100hrs on October 3, Miles turned to bombardment. While the Hotchkiss cannon fired from the southwest, the 12-pdr lobbed in projectiles from the west. Miles had only a limited ammunition stock so the bombardment was sporadic, but it inflicted some casualties on the noncombatants and began to demoralize the Nez Perce. The bombardment commenced again on October 4, as hunger and cold also began to bite into Nez Perce resolve. Around 1700hrs, Howard and two-dozen cavalry rode into Miles's headquarters; Howard left Miles in command of the operation but sent dispatches calling for more reinforcements.

Another ceasefire went into effect at 0800hrs on October 5 and negotiations were soon under way. On the understanding that his people would be taken to the Lapwai Reservation, Joseph agreed to surrender and appeared in front of Miles and Howard at 1440hrs. He gave a short speech, which supposedly included the famous conclusion to the war: "Hear me, my chiefs. I am tired, my heart is sick and sad. From where the sun now stands I will fight no more forever." After that, Joseph was taken into custody and both his band and the Palouse began to file out of the ravine and surrender their arms. A total of 418 Nez Perce – including 87 warriors, 184 squaws and 147 children – were taken into army custody. Another 30 refugees were rounded up in the next few days. However, not all the Nez Perce were willing to surrender. White Bird and Yellow Wolf waited until nightfall with about 50 of their people and then began exfiltrating northward along Snake Creek, ignominiously abandoning the bulk of their noncombatants. Although White Bird and Yellow Wolf made it to Canada, along with about 105 Nez Perce warriors and 70–100 noncombatants, many other refugees from the battle of Bear Paw were hunted down and killed by local Indian tribes, who were rewarded with tobacco by the US Army. Even Looking Glass, the inveterate warrior, was caught on the flat plains north of Bear Paw and killed by a Cheyenne scout, as was U-em-till-lilp-cown, the last of the warriors responsible for the murders in Idaho. After 113 days and the longest pursuit in US Army history, the Nez Perce campaign was over.

AFTERMATH

After the surrender at Bear Paw, Miles escorted the Nez Perce prisoners to the Tongue River cantonment and, after a brief stay, they were sent south to Fort Leavenworth where they spent the next eight months. Although Howard and Miles had both promised Joseph that the Nez Perce would be returned to Idaho, Gen. Sherman was adamant that they be punished severely and he prevailed upon Congress to deport them to the Indian Territory (Oklahoma). In July 1878, the Nez Perce arrived in the Indian Territory, where they were forced to become indifferent farmers for the next seven years. Exile was hard on the Nez Perce, with over 150 dying from disease in the first two years. It was not until 1883 that a small number of Nez Perce was allowed to return to the Lapwai Reservation and the remainder in 1885. Once they returned to Lapwai, the Treaty Nez Perce generally shunned them.

Nor did the Nez Perce who escaped to Canada fare very well. Although Sitting Bull and the Sioux accepted them, most were soon reduced to semi-starvation and suffered terribly from the cold. Sanctuary in Canada proved to be a chimera, lacking in either hope or freedom. Most of the refugees opted to return to the United States by 1881 and quietly made their way back to Lapwai. Only a few holdouts like White Bird refused to yield, but a fellow Nez Perce murdered him in Canada in 1892.

Although the Nez Perce lost the military campaign, they did very well in the postwar propaganda campaign. Even before the end of the war, Eastern newspapers such as the *New York Times* and *Harper's Weekly* were referring to Joseph as "the Red Napoleon" because of his supposed military skills. However, the eastern press was ignorant of the fact that Joseph was not responsible for Nez Perce military successes or that the Nez Perce had missed opportunities that the real Napoleon would never have let slip. The press also lauded Joseph and the Nez Perce for their "clean" manner of warfare, claiming that they didn't kill wounded and spared women and children. In fact, the Nez Perce had fought a savage and brutal campaign, rarely taking prisoners and murdering noncombatants across three territories. Joseph made two visits to the east and won wide sympathy but he was not allowed to return to the Wallowa Valley and in 1885 he was sent to the Colville Reservation in northeast Washington.

The Nez Perce campaign was a very difficult one for the US Army, fought over rough terrain, at great distances from its sources of supply and in a multijurisdictional environment that inhibited unity of command. The US Army suffered a total of 112 deaths and 132 wounded during the Nez Perce campaign, or about 13 percent of the forces involved in the pursuit.

Joseph and his family at Fort Leavenworth in Kansas after his surrender. He was exiled to Oklahoma and was eventually allowed to return to the Colville Reservation in Washington, but not the Lapwai Reservation or the Wallowa Valley. (Washington State Historical Society)

In comparison, the Nez Perce suffered at least 75 out of 250 warriors killed in the campaign, plus another 40–50 noncombatant deaths. Other American casualties included 12 armed volunteers killed in action and 36 civilians murdered in Nez Perce raids. The Nez Perce campaign was the longest pursuit operation in US military history, with elements of the 1st Cavalry and 21st Infantry marching over 1,630 miles (2,620km) in three months. Yet despite the fact that the Nez Perce were on the run for 107 days, they were seriously pressed by the army on only a few occasions – which contributed to their sense of complacency at Big Hole and Bear Paw. Howard's pursuit was on-again/off-again and never really seriously threatened the Nez Perce with annihilation, even at the Clearwater. Indeed, Howard's forces killed only a grand total of four Nez Perce. Despite later claims that the Nez Perce had fought against long odds, the US Army was never able to achieve better than a two-to-one numerical superiority against them on the battlefield and actually fought outnumbered or at parity on most other occasions.

Howard's poor performance during the Nez Perce campaign encouraged unrest among other tribes in his district, beginning with the Bannocks in southern Idaho and the Paiutes in eastern Oregon. The trouble began barely a month after Joseph's surrender when a Bannock killed an American near the

Fort Hall Reservation. Howard dispatched troops to arrest the murderer and this led to further unrest on the reservation. Throughout the winter of 1877–78 the troops kept close guard on the situation but in May 1878, Chief Buffalo Horn led a mixed force of 200 Bannocks, Paiutes and Umatillas off the reservation and they went on a killing spree in southern Idaho, murdering 10 American civilians. Buffalo Horn had been a scout for the US Army during the Nez Perce campaign and he was familiar with army tactics, so he headed west into Oregon to link up with the friendly Paiute tribe. Although Buffalo Horn was killed in a skirmish with civilian volunteers, his group succeeded in uniting with the Paiutes and together they had about 450 warriors and 300 noncombatants.

Howard's response to the Bannock–Paiute coalition was virtually a carbon copy of his plan of operations against the Nez Perce. While sending a battalion of the 1st Cavalry in pursuit, he tried to get the 21st Infantry in place as a blocking force. Although he assumed direct command of the pursuit, Howard was blessed with more competent subordinates this time and the 1st Cavalry succeeded in surprising and scattering the Bannock–Paiute camps in a series of raids. About 600 Paiutes eventually surrendered in August but a group of Bannocks tried to emulate the Nez Perce and slipped eastward through Yellowstone National Park, hoping to reach Canada. This time however, Col. Nelson A Miles was waiting with just 35 soldiers at Clark's Fork Canyon and he conducted a textbook ambush that effectively ended the campaign.

The following year, Howard had to send the 1st Cavalry in again during the Sheepeater War (May–October 1879), to suppress a small tribe of renegades who were murdering prospectors along the Salmon River. The Sheepeater War was the last Indian campaign in the Pacific Northwest and ended with the surrender of the renegades. Although Howard's reputation was somewhat restored by the campaigns of 1878–79, he never completely overcame allegations of incompetence during the Nez Perce campaign and Joseph's speech in Washington, DC, in 1879 blamed Howard for instigating the war. Howard also wrecked his friendship with Nelson Miles by arguing over the credit for capturing Joseph. Miles was in fact the primary beneficiary of the Nez Perce campaign, receiving his promotion to brigadier-general three years later and eventually rising to commanding general of the US Army in 1895 – a remarkable career for a non-West Point officer.

THE BATTLEFIELDS TODAY

The US National Park Service administers the Nez Perce National Historical Park, which consists of 38 sites spread across the states of Idaho, Oregon, Wyoming and Montana. Flying into Boise, Idaho, I headed north along routes 55 and 95 to the Salmon River area where the Nez Perce Campaign started. The White Bird Canyon battlefield is right off Route 95 but virtually untouched by any development from the nearby town. There is no visitor center here or park rangers, but visitors can acquire a brochure at the gated entrance for a self-guided tour along the 1½-mile-long (2km) walking trail that terminates at McCarthy Point. There are also six colored historical panels along the trail to highlight key moments in the battle. After years of walking 'touristy' battlefields like Gettysburg, Waterloo and Normandy, it's interesting to walk across the battlefield at White Bird Canyon since so little has changed since 1877 and there is not a gift shop in sight. Instead, on the windy ridgeline, you get a great feel for what both Capt. Perry and the Nez

Bear Paw battlefield at dawn. There are a number of markers erected to honor both sides, but the fallen soldiers are buried at the military cemetery at Little Bighorn. Despite the fact that five Medals of Honor were awarded for heroism at this action, Bear Paw has become one of America's forgotten battlefields. (Author's collection)

Grave of Corporal John Haddoo, Company B, 5th Infantry, who was killed in action at Bear Paw on September 30, 1877. (Author's collection)

Perce leaders could see from their respective viewpoints. Visitors should be prepared for a taxing uphill climb to the cliff at McCarthy's Point and mindful of the rattlesnake threat in summer months. Visiting the site of Lt. Theller's last stand, it is disappointing to see that the Park Service has failed to erect any marker for his troops or any of the 34 soldiers killed in the battle. Along Route 95 and the Salmon River, there are a number of historical markers related to the Nez Perce campaign, but none that mentions the 18 citizens murdered here in June 1877.

Driving northward, you can head toward either the Cottonwood (of which the battlefield is now covered up by modern housing) and the Lapwai Agency or toward the Clearwater River. At Lapwai, which is still the center of the Nez Perce Reservation, there are a number of sites related to the original missionaries, but of less relevance to the 1877 campaign. The Clearwater battlefield is located on a ridgeline just east of modern Stites, Idaho. Unlike the other major battlefields of the Nez Perce campaign, Clearwater is primarily on private land and inaccessible. There is a single historical marker for the battle, but otherwise negligible help from the Park Service. The site of the Nez Perce village on the Clearwater is accessible, as is the site of Looking Glass's camp, a few miles north. At Stites, the Clearwater River is quite shallow and it's hard to see why Howard had such difficulty fording this obstacle. It is possible to drive up part of Battle Ridge where Howard maneuvered his forces and it is clear that this was virtually "no-go" terrain for his artillery and Gatling guns. When I visited I proceeded northeastward up Route 12, paralleling the Lolo Trail, for about 100 miles (160km). This is rough but breathtaking terrain even today and it makes one wonder what would have happened if either side had been ambushed in this chokepoint.

After crossing the Lolo Pass, I stopped at Fort Fizzle, not far from Missoula, Montana. The Park Service has a few historical panels here and a reconstruction of one of the rifle pits. The actual rifle pits disappeared decades ago but it is still possible to appreciate Capt. Rawn's predicament in trying to hold this pathetic effort at fieldworks. After Missoula, I headed south into the

Bitterroot Valley toward the Big Hole, which is a proper historical site, complete with visitor center and Park Service guides wearing Smokey the Bear hats. The visitor center has a 12-pdr mountain howitzer on display, as well as a number or artifacts dug up on the battlefield. Visitors should be advised that the history presented at this site is biased toward the Nez Perce perspective. Interestingly, there is no mention of the Dreamer movement and how this contributed to the war. I headed over to the actual battlefield, which is extremely well preserved. Pamphlets are available for a self-guided $1^{1}/_{4}$-mile-long (2km) walking tour of the "Siege Area," where there is a monument listing US casualties, the area from which Gibbon's attack was launched and the 12-pdr howitzer site. The Nez Perce village is marked by a series of "ghostly" tepees with lodge poles but no covering.

Although the Nez Perce Trail dips down into Wyoming, there is relatively little to see at Camas Meadows, other than some rocky rifle pits erected by Captain Norwood's men, and it may not be worth the additional mileage. There are a few markers along these parts of the trail, including one at Canyon Creek, but the main final site is Bear Paw, near modern Chinook, Montana. The Park Service administers the Bear Paw battlefield and provides pamphlets for a self-guided walking tour on the $1^{1}/_{4}$-mile-long (2km) trail, but there is no visitor center there. Several organizations have erected markers at Bear Paw, including one listing US Army casualties, most of whom are buried in the cemetery at the Little Bighorn battlefield. The Nez Perce have placed markers where specific warriors such as Ollokot were killed, as well as the location of Joseph's lodge. As I was there on the 132nd anniversary of the surrender, a park ranger was present but the commemoration consisted entirely of a speech given by a Nez Perce delegation.

FURTHER READING

Cozzens, Peter, *Eyewitnesses to the Indian Wars 1865–1890, Volume 2* Stackpole
    Books: Mechanicsburg, PA, 2002

Greene, Jerome A., *Nez Perce Summer 1877* Helena Historical Society Press:
    Helena, MT, 2000

Haines, Aubrey L., *The Battle of Big Hole* Two Dot Books: Helena, MT, 2007

Highberger Mark, *The Death of Wind Blowing* Bear Creek Press: Wallowa,
    OR: 2000

Laughy, Linwood, *In Pursuit of the Nez Perces* Mountain Meadow Press: Kooskia,
    ID, 2002

Josephy Jr., Alvin M., *The Nez Perce Indians and the Opening of the Northwest*
    Yale University Press: New Haven, CT, 1965

McDermott, John D., *Forlorn Hope: The Nez Perce Victory at White Bird Canyon*
    Caxton Press: Caldwell, ID, 2003

Utley, Robert M., *Frontier Regulars: The United States Army and the Indian,
    1866–90* Macmillan Publishing Co.: New York, 1973

West, Elliott, *The Last Indian War: The Nez Perce Story* Oxford University Press:
    New York, 2009

Wooster, Robert, *Nelson A. Miles and The Twilight of the Frontier Army* The
    University of Nebraska Press: Lincoln, NE, 1993

INDEX

Numbers in **bold** refer to plates, maps and illustrations.